WHOLE LIFE WELL-BEING

7 ESSENTIAL ELEMENTS

BESTSELLING AUTHOR

FATIMA DOMAN

ACCOLADES

"I highly recommend Fatima Doman's new book, *Whole Life Well-Being*! Everyone should learn how to use their character strengths to recharge all essential aspects of their well-being. The tools in this book can shift one's mindset to look more for the highest and best in themselves and others—increasing overall well-being. A must-read in today's era of rising stress, depression, and anxiety."

—**Daniel G. Amen, MD**, 12x New York Times #1 bestselling author

"In her new book, *Whole Life Well-Being*, Fatima Doman has leveraged the science of positive psychology to provide a brilliantly accessible toolbox for leading a happier, more successful, and more fulfilling life. This is an important book for you—if you are interested in making the most of your gifts and talents, and in boosting your well-being!"

—**Dr. Tal Ben-Shahar**, #1 bestselling author of *Happier* and *Choose the Life You Want*

"In this jewel of a book, *Whole Life Well-Being*, Fatima Doman lays out simple, research-based tools for developing the seven essential elements of well-being that we all need, especially in these most trying times. Brilliant, wise, and a masterful teacher and storyteller, Doman is one of the bright lights in positive psychology, well-being and human flourishing. A must-read for anyone wanting to live a meaningful and thriving life!"

—**Joan Borysenko PhD**, bestselling author of *Minding the Body, Mending the Mind*

"This book will help you build well-being in a deceptively simple, yet transformative way—by learning to become your inner ally rather than being your own worst enemy!"

—**Dr. Kristin Neff**, bestselling author of *Self-Compassion*, associate professor, University of Texas at Austin

"This ground-breaking book is a must-read to boost your well-being. In today's era of increasing stress, this book is a significant contribution to the rapidly exploding field of positive psychology and the development of well-being within each reader. Rooted in the 'science of happiness' and based upon the study of character strengths, *Whole Life Well-Being* lays out a road map to recharge each of the seven essential elements of well-being that is both practical and easy to implement. Essential for all of us striving to live a meaningful, productive, and vibrant life!"

—**Dr. Sandra Scheinbaum**, founder and CEO, Functional Medicine Coaching Academy, Inc., author of *Functional Medicine Coaching*

"Applying the evidence-based, 'whole life' principles in this book will help you discover and leverage your strengths to boost your well-being, improve your relationships, and fulfill your potential to flourish—and help others do the same!"

—**Stephen M.R. Covey**, #1 bestselling author of *The Speed of Trust* and *Smart Trust*

"Fatima Doman has written a wonderful book! Thorough and wise, it is a road map for well-being and growth. I found it comprehensive in its reach, yet easy to relate to, and spot-on in advice quality."

—**Dr. Fredrick Luskin**, director of Stanford Forgiveness Project, Stanford University

"In 2012, I became paraplegic in a matter of seconds. I struggled with depression and PTSD. My life as I knew it was over and I had no control. Wrong! Fatima Doman showed me that my strengths had always been within and my capacity to bounce back as well. Fatima's new book, *Whole Life Well-Being: 7 Essential Elements*, like her previous books, inspires and guides us to the realization that we are each powerful. Our well-being is within and Fatima helps us find the way. Her capacity to explain and concretize concepts from positive psychology makes it easy to carve our own path to well-being!"

—**Marjorie Aunos PhD**, psychologist and survivor

"Fatima Doman's books are profoundly helpful and applicable to the current global situation! I believe her new book, Whole Life Well-Being, will also bring significant benefits to people who read it."

—**Darvin Widjaja**, founder and CEO, Reignite Consulting Group, Indonesia

"Congratulations, Fatima Doman, on creating another book that not only educates but uplifts! A large part of positive psychology is about the journey to uncover your authentic self. *Whole Life Well-Being* is a great evidence-based guide for cultivating well-being. A must-have for your positive psychology library."

—**Dr. Suzy Green, D Psych (Clin) MAPS,**
founder and CEO, the Positivity Institute

"We've all had the experience of reading a book and not wanting to put it away for even a second. Fatima Doman's new book, *Whole Life Well-Being*, is one of those readings. A book that you will want to read again and again, and to ask all the ones you love to do the same! It's both the science of living a good life and the practical tools to make it happen. If, like me, you want all that life has to offer, you must have this book at your side!"

—**Henrique Bueno**, MsC Positive Psychology, CEO and
founder of Wholebeing Institute Brasil

"Fatima Doman and I met two years ago when we invited her to Romania to teach *Authentic Strengths* to our school. Our entire philosophy is built around growing through healthy relationships and learning to acknowledge one's strengths by understanding core needs and emotions. Fatima's contribution to our school mindset was significant, and we are grateful we met her and benefited from her knowledge. We wish her work will expand to many state schools and communities in Romania and throughout Europe, to help children and adults live a thriving life, empowering the next generation!"

—**Ruxandra Mercea**, executive headteacher, Transylvania College,
and co-founder of The Cambridge International School in Cluj & Wellbeing Institute

"Fatima Doman has done it again! She has written a book that is highly relevant for anyone and everyone who wants to increase their well-being. This book addresses the 'whole person' and applies the latest science to common life experiences in an easily understandable manner. More people would feel whole and thrive if they read this book!"

—**Dr. Chelsea Shields**, anthropologist, TEDx speaker, and former TED Fellow

"It isn't often that a book can both educate and inspire. *Whole Life Well-Being* doesn't just succeed at these, it super-succeeds! Fatima Doman takes research and humanizes it, breathing life into it by telling personal stories and providing engaging exercises. I was captivated by Fatima Doman's sharp mind, compassionate heart, and inspiring energy. You will be transformed by this book!"

—**Dr. Everett L. Worthington**, professor emeritus, Virginia Commonwealth University, founder of the REACH Forgiveness Program

"Experiencing wholeness—a sense of opening to all that you are—is helped along when you look at this human life through multiple lenses. Different perspectives give a new view of you. Through her organized model, Fatima Doman generously lays out opportunities to explore these facets of self. This book is a gem!"

—**Megan McDonough**, author and founder, Wholebeing Institute

"*Whole Life Well-Being* is the book I've been searching for my whole life! Fatima Doman's soothing voice and years of expertise shine through every page. Discover the power of positive psychology and how to step into your AWESOMENESS with this new masterpiece. You won't want to put it down!"

—**Nathan Osmond**, keynote speaker, entertainer, and host of "Achieving Awesomeness Now" podcast

"Praises to Fatima Doman for creating such an inspiring and hopeful book at a time where leaders, employees, parents, and all people in general are feeling overwhelmed with things we feel are out of our control. Thank you for refocusing us on seven essentials within our sphere of control and laying out how each of us can utilize our character strengths to navigate life, increasing our effectiveness and happiness overall. *Whole Life Well-Being* is a must-read for anyone choosing to lead their life using tools we already possess! Fatima graciously walks us through the *what, why,* and *how* of how to use the character strengths we all have to 'recharge' our whole life experience with genuine well-being."

—**Dr. Felicia Alley English**, Human & Organizational Development Consultant & Coach

"Leveraging the science of positive psychology, *Whole Life Well-Being* is transformational! In today's world of uncertainty and constant change, this book provides practical ways to apply this exciting science in everyday life, in a simplified and accessible manner. A must-read for anyone interested in boosting their well-being to flourish!"

—**David M.R. Covey**, CEO of SMCOVEY and
bestselling co-author of: *Trap Tales: Outsmarting the 7 Obstacles to Success*

"*Whole Life Well-Being* is a must read! Be brilliantly guided by Fatima Doman's accessible tools based on evidence-based research and practical wisdom. The way you think of well-being will be forever changed. Absolutely essential!"

—**Stephan Mardyks**, CEO, Wisdom Destinations®

"Fatima Doman has brilliantly encapsulated the concept of well-being within its seven essential elements. I personally believe spirit binds the rest of the other six elements since an inward journey will set the path for one's life to achieve holistic well-being. Hence, a good read to transform one's life wholesomely!"

—**Asohan Satkunasingham**, award-winning author, Progressive Human Resource
Practitioner, and High Impact Corporate Trainer, Malaysia

"This new book, *Whole Life Well-Being,* is a necessary read for practitioners, educators, parents, and students—anyone wanting to explore strengths to build well-being, resilience, and truly capitalize on the value of individuals. We become better leaders, parents, and students as we learn skills to empower ourselves, and our influence will grow as we apply the principles in this book. Doman provides fresh insight and practical application that gives clarity to the science behind positive psychology and well-being. Each chapter is personally and professionally inspiring."

—**Dr. Jaynee Poulson**, former Utah State PTA Health Commissioner,
professor at Weber State University

"Life is complicated. Or is it? As I was reading *Whole Life Well-Being* by Fatima Doman, I couldn't help but ask the question to myself repeatedly: 'Do I make things complicated by not focusing on the seven elements in this book?' Just like a world-class physical fitness trainer motivates the athlete, so does Fatima to the reader. She lays out the seven elements with such precision and clarity, encouraging you in such a profound way that you will want to embrace the Whole Life Well-Being model as she teaches it!"

—**David T. Williams**, COO, Blaze Performance Solutions

"*Whole Life Well-Being* provides a unique perspective and a new set of tools that each person can use to improve their life. It's a must-read for anyone wanting to explore cutting-edge ways to increase their well-being."

—**Michael Hunter, PhD**, founder and CEO, Healthcare Improvement Sciences, LLC

"*Whole Life Well-Being* is a remarkable book that introduces people to the transformational world of character strengths, and their role in recharging our well-being. Research continues to show the profound, positive benefits that character strengths have on our lives. Truly, this book is a gift to us all!"

—**Tiffany Yoast, MEd**, Utah Valley University

"People all over the world are looking for well-being, meaning, and purpose in their lives. *Whole Life Well-Being* by Fatima Doman is a breath of fresh air and outlines how to live a more uplifting and thriving life. I highly recommend this book as it provides ideas on a more powerful way of living!"

—**Trish Barrus, PhD**, author of *10 Principles of Recovery*

"We live in a critical stage of humanity's cultural development. What I call the 'integrality of being' has to do not only with having a healthier and more satisfying personal life, it is also an adaptative requirement for our species to the present and future challenges of our existence. Fatima Doman understands the 'how to do' of such a vital transition better than most thinkers and researchers of our time."

—**Luciano Alves Meira**, author and co-founder of Caminhos Vida Integral

WHOLE LIFE WELL-BEING

7 ESSENTIAL ELEMENTS

BESTSELLING AUTHOR

FATIMA DOMAN

Published in the United States by Authentic Strengths Advantage, LLC
www.AuthenticStrengths.com
Copyright © Fatima Doman 2021
All rights reserved.

This title is also available in an e-book via Authentic Strengths Advantage, LLC
ISBN: 978-1-7348688-3-8
Library of Congress Control Number: 2021912143
Printed in the United States of America

Note to the Reader: Throughout these pages, some names and identifying features within stories have been changed to preserve confidentiality.

Disclaimer: Every effort has been made by the author and the publisher to ensure that the information contained in this book is complete and accurate. The content is based on the personal and coaching experiences of the author and those of clients, colleagues, friends and family, in addition to an extensive review of relevant research. It is published for general reference and education with the intent of inspiring hope, increasing well-being, boosting resilience, and offering encouragement.

Warning: The information in all Authentic Strengths Advantage, LLC (ASA®), programs, content, books, website, microlearning or e-learning, by necessity, is of a general nature and is not a substitute for an evaluation or treatment by a competent mental health or medical practitioner. If you believe you or anyone you coach, or share this content with, is in need of physical or psychological interventions, that person should contact a medical practitioner as soon as possible. There are no guaranteed results whatsoever, expressed or implied. Any communication with, or information received from ASA® or anyone affiliated with ASA® shall not, under any circumstance, constitute mental, emotional, or physical health, career, leadership, personal leadership, or legal advice. All information herein is provided "AS IS" and ASA® makes no warranties, express or implied, or otherwise, regarding the accuracy, completeness, or performance of said information. This book is sold with the understanding that neither the author, nor publisher, is engaged in rendering any professional services including legal, psychological, career, wellness, or medical advice to the individual reader. The author and publisher, as well as ASA®, its parent, affiliates, directors, officers, members, coaches, trainers, shareholders, employees, associates, distributors, licensees, successors, and/or assigns hereby disclaim any and all liability for damages, losses, or injuries of any kind or nature whatsoever, arising out of, resulting from, or in any way connected to anyone's use of, or reliance upon ASA® content, books, audios, videos, coaching, training, certification, website, microlearning, e-learning, communications, social media, or correspondence. Neither the author nor the publisher assumes responsibility for errors, inaccuracies, omissions, or inconsistencies.

For all of those seeking joy in the journey.
May you find inspiration to invest in yourselves and in your relationships—
creating vibrant well-being along the way.

Jessica,
Let your strengths be seen. They are inspiring.

Patricia Donovan

CONTENTS

INTRODUCTION

WELCOME!

I'm enthusiastic to share with you what I've learned about the seven essential elements of well-being. The elements we will explore are based on timeless principles that enhance the quality of our lives and our relationships. The principles are grounded in scientific research and have been shown to increase one's overall well-being, resiliency, energy, engagement, achievement, happiness, fulfillment, and more!

So, what do I mean by "whole life well-being"? Search dictionaries for "wholeness" and you will find: "the state of forming a complete and harmonious whole; unity,"[1] or "the quality of being whole or complete."[2] Next, let's look at "well-being," defined as: "the state of being comfortable, healthy, or happy,"[3] or "the condition of an individual...for example their social, economic, psychological, spiritual, or medical state...high well-being is positive...low well-being is negative..."[4] In addition, Dr. Martin Seligman, known for ushering in the scientific field of positive psychology, identified well-being as having five core elements known by the acronym: "PERMA." PERMA stands for: Positive Emotions, Engagement, Relationships, Meaning/Purpose, and Accomplishment.[5] The World Health Organization (WHO), points to the significance of the many aspects of well-being in their constitution as follows: "Health is a state of complete physical, mental and social well-being and not merely the absence of disease or infirmity."[6]

Therefore, we can understand "whole life well-being" as a whole person living a whole, healthy, and happy life made up of positive emotions, engagement, positive relationships, meaning, purpose, and accomplishment. Sounds great, doesn't it? So how do we create more of this in our lives?

In this book, we will focus on each of the seven elements at a time—supported by studies that address the many areas of well-being. For example, we will explore how our well-being can be supported or diminished by the environments we live and work in, by our sense of abundance in our lives, by our care for our physical bodies and vitality, by our relationships with self and others, by our unique contributions to the world around us, by how we use and expand our mind, and culminating with the highest expression of our spirit—our inward journey to the greatness within each of us. It's when we consider our "whole" selves and our "whole" lives that we can enjoy all-encompassing well-being—living in harmony with the many aspects of our being.

As you learn about each of these seven elements of well-being, you will tap into your character strengths, that core part of yourself that energizes and recharges you.

100 YEARS OF WELL-BEING

Meet my dear friend Lucy Dettmer on her 100th birthday, celebrating online with friends right in the midst of the COVID-19 pandemic! Her love of party hats undiminished, Lucy has always said: "A birthday party without hats is just a meeting!" She's an inspiring example of well-being.

It's encouraging to see people embrace aging with positivity, courage, and a connection to others. Studies have demonstrated that people with positive attitudes tend to live longer and enjoy greater well-being than those plagued with negativity about getting older.[7]

I asked Lucy: to what does she attribute her long life and vibrancy? The biggest factor, said Lucy: "always dwell on the positive." Her philosophy is "pick the good stuff, don't mess around with the rest." Lucy intentionally seeks out positive people and inspiring literature, art, movies, and activities. She also is authentic, in her own words: "Some people work so hard to create a persona, and it isn't really their true self."

When Lucy lost her husband of sixty-five years, she challenged herself to transcend her overwhelming loneliness by getting out and helping people: "Everyone experiences loss, and you have to figure out how you handle it...You can't wait for good things to fall into your lap—you've got to go out and find the good things." And Lucy does just that. She and her daughter Peggy continue to volunteer in causes that help others.

I have great memories of hiking with Lucy well into her 90s. She would stop and take in all the scenery—pointing out the beauty around us—the blooming sweet peas, the Indian paintbrush, the buttercups. I watched her closely in those moments of deep appreciation for her surroundings, and it's as though every cell in her body soaked in the positivity. She looked so energized, alive, and youthful during those times.

What's Lucy's secret to well-being, now in her hundredth year of life? What makes her so special? Can each of us develop Lucy's character strengths of gratitude, appreciation of beauty, hope, zest, perseverance, bravery, etc.? Lucy thinks we can. Even better, these attributes are learnable, so we can boost our well-being at any age!

OUR ROADMAP

Here's our "roadmap" for our journey together. First, you will learn the "what, why, and how" of character strengths as they relate to your well-being: **what** they are, **why** they matter, and **how** you can use them to recharge your whole life well-being.

Next, you will dive into each of the seven essential elements of well-being, one-by-one: **environment**, **abundance**, **body**, **heart**, **contribution**, **mind**, and **spirit**. You will explore practical tools and use mindfulness-based strengths practices (known as "MBSP")[8] to invigorate each important element of your life. You will engage in fun exercises that bring these concepts to life for *sustainable* positive change—which is dependent upon your sense of well-being in all these aspects of your life. Lastly, you will have opportunities to reflect and apply the learning in your own life.

In caring for the seven essential elements of your well-being on a regular basis, you will honor your wholeness. You won't just haphazardly pay attention to the parts of your life that are currently screaming out for attention, but instead you will proactively nurture your "whole life," recognizing this as the most important gift you can give to yourself.

THE "POSITIVE" DIFFERENCE

Positive psychology is the study of human flourishing and well-being. It focuses on a person's individual strengths to help people feel and do their best in all aspects of life: home, school, work, relationships, communities, etc. Many highly regarded universities conduct research in the fields of positive psychology and well-being that is referenced in this book. I've drawn from an extensive body of research to create powerful well-being tools for you. Since positive psychology is a predominant science behind well-being, let's take a closer look.

So, what is positive psychology? Dr. Martin Seligman, the father of the positive psychology movement, explained in his groundbreaking books, *Authentic Happiness* and *Flourish,* that once we know what our best qualities are, they open up a vital pathway to thriving. Due to the science of positive psychology (which focuses on what's strong about a person) vs. the traditional psychology problem-focused approach (which focuses on what's wrong with a person), we now can identify the strengths that define who we are at our best—the qualities that, when nurtured, can lead to good outcomes in every area of our lives.[9]

What we choose to focus on grows and directly impacts our well-being. We can choose to focus on what's wrong with ourselves and our lives, and that list will grow. Conversely, we can choose to focus on what's strong and best in ourselves and in our lives (our strengths), and that list will become the trajectory for our lives. Which do you choose?

Below is a real-life, inspiring example of a woman named Marjorie Aunos, who chose to focus on what's strong, even in the face of tremendous trials. Marjorie sent me the following:

> At 34 years old, I was a hardworking-strong-willed-perfectionistic-career-oriented-psychologist-and-single-mother-by-choice of a toddler. I was grateful for having achieved most of my life goals. But when a severe accident rendered me paraplegic, I lost all my bearings. I felt profoundly hopeless and powerless. I was left with an emptiness that things were left unfinished. I needed to find something to hold onto...that's when I learned about character strengths. This new outlook literally saved my life.
>
> With positive psychology, the focus was NOT on my diagnoses. Not on my depression or PTSD. The focus was on my own strengths. What I *could do*. What made me strong and resilient. This is what I desperately needed, and it was inside of me.
>
> I feel I survived my accident because I love my son so much, giving me a strong desire to live. Heck, I thought love was an emotion... so when I realized that love was one of my top character strengths, I got the validation I was looking for.
>
> All of a sudden, I felt empowered. The accident didn't just "happen" to me, I could grow from it. You may have guessed, another one of my top strengths is love of learning. As I read and researched, I was able to crawl out of that dark hole I had fallen into. It was clear. I was able to say I was loving, a lifelong learner, and perseverant—I was strong. I saw how using my strength of humor helped me mentally survive some of the most embarrassing moments in recovery, how building on my strength of teamwork with my parents got us to a place where we could co-parent my son together for his benefit.

We drew on our love for one another to achieve this. I could see how my strengths of hope, appreciation for beauty and excellence, and gratitude infused my life with positive emotions and gave me relief on the bleakest of days. Knowing how to tap into my character strengths also led me to finding solace and peace in mindfulness practices, and most importantly, has given me hope.[10]

Marjorie found her own inner, unshakable core strengths—something to which she could anchor her wildly tossing boat of life. When we learn to strategically call upon our strengths, we can move beyond just surviving life's challenges to enjoying expansive benefits in our lives—giving us a new lease on life. We know from positive psychology research that these four things are true about character strengths:

- First, they are positive traits all humans possess.
- Second, they are universally valued, meaning that they are valued in all cultures around the world.
- Third, character strengths are expressed in varying degrees, or at different levels. For example, one person may be very high in expressing courage, whereas another person may be more moderate in expressing courage.
- And fourth, they are learnable! The exciting news is that anyone can learn how to express any of the 24 character strengths more fully at any time.[11]

A DEEPER DIVE

Let's go even deeper into understanding character strengths and how they can boost your well-being. Leveraging your character strengths is a powerful way to recharge all seven essential elements of your well-being. In fact, hundreds of studies around the world show that using character strengths results in:

- More energy and an elevated sense of well-being
- Greater resilience and reduced stress
- People report feeling happier
- Engagement and achievement increases
- More fulfilling and positive relationships overall[12]

VIA CHARACTER STRENGTHS

Paying attention to and making the most of your character strengths is associated with a number of positive health behaviors that promote well-being, such as living a physically active life, engaging in healthy nutrition habits, bouncing back from disappointments, expanding your mind with new learning, pursuing enjoyable activities, valuing relationships—the list goes on and on. Furthermore, these strengths have been highly correlated with well-being subscales of self-acceptance and purpose, as well as good physical and mental health.[13] People who make strong use of their character strengths tend to experience greater well-being overall.[14] Below is a brief overview of the 24 VIA character strengths, categorized into six "virtue categories":

Wisdom	CREATIVITY • Orinality • Ingenuity	CURIOSITY • Interest • Openness	JUDGMENT • Open-Mindedness • Rational Thinking	LOVE OF LEARNING • Interest in Gaining Knowledge	PERSPECTIVE • Wisdom • Big Picture View
Courage	BRAVERY • Courage • Valor	PERSEVERANCE • Persistence • Industriousness	HONESTY • Authenticity • Integrity	ZEST • Vitality/Enthusiasm • Energy/Vigor	
Humanity	LOVE • Loving/Being Loved • Close Relationships	KINDNESS • Generosity/Nurturance • Care/Compassion			SOCIAL INTELLIGENCE • Emotional Awareness • Relationship Intelligence
Justice	TEAMWORK • Citizenship/Loyalty • Social Responsibility			FAIRNESS • Just • Not Biased	LEADERSHIP • Organizer • Encourager of a Group
Temperance		FORGIVENESS • Mercy • Letting Go	HUMILITY • Modesty • Humbleness	PRUDENCE • Careful/Cautious • Practical Reason	SELF-REGULATION • Self-Control • Disciplined
Transcendence	APPRECIATION OF BEAUTY & EXCELLENCE • Awe/Wonder • Elevation	GRATITUDE • Appreciation • Feeling Blessed	HOPE • Optimism • Future-Mindedness	HUMOR • Playfulness • Lighthearted	SPIRITUALITY • Faith • Purpose

The VIA Survey of Character Strengths is a scientifically valid, peer-reviewed tool that helps you to focus on what's strong in your life instead of on what's wrong. For example, the survey might show your top strengths as being qualities like leadership, kindness, humor, perspective and creativity. *All 24 of the VIA Character Strengths matter equally. No one strength is more important than another.* You can discover your own unique strengths profile by visiting AuthenticStrengths.com and taking the free survey—it only takes about ten minutes.[15]

YOUR TOP STRENGTHS

Some strengths are more strongly represented in you (and therefore will rise to the top of your strengths report) and are core to your identity—to who you are. These are called your "signature strengths," or "top strengths." Your top strengths are like your fingerprint because they define your uniqueness and represent your authentic self. These top strengths are those that feel almost as natural to you as breathing. You likely feel energized and satisfied when you are expressing them. And when others see them in you, you feel understood in an important way. If you are unable to express these parts of yourself for some reason, you might feel like you are suffocating or dying inside. That's why focusing on your top strengths and how to put them into play—at work, at school, and in life—is so important.

As you look at your strengths survey results, and in particular your top strengths, ask yourself these questions to determine whether a character strength is truly a top strength for you. Write down your answers to these questions in your *Whole Life Well-Being Workbook* that accompanies this book (or you can make your own worbook):

- Is this character strength authentic?
- Does it show up often?
- Do others notice it?
- Does using it energize you?
- If unable to express it, would you feel empty?

Your VIA report shows a ranking of your 24 character strengths with your most-used strengths at the top, and your less-used strengths at the bottom. Take the next few minutes to review your report and become familiar with it so that you can do the next step, which will be to create a snapshot of your strengths. *(It's important to note that lower ranked scores do not indicate a "weakness." These are called "less-used strengths," which means the individual does not express these strengths as often as their top strengths. For example, scoring low on honesty does not mean that a person lies a lot. The VIA scale does not assess lying or dishonesty at all. A lower score/ranking simply means that for that individual they have other strengths that are more dominant in their life. A person who scores low on honesty may, **or may not**, lie a lot.)*

If you would like more information about the many aspects of character strengths (this book offers only a brief introduction), you can find a more in-depth exploration of character strengths in my book, *Authentic Resilience*.

ARE YOU LISTENING TO YOUR INNER CRITIC OR YOUR INNER COACH?

With this knowledge of character strengths, let's now do an activity about your inner mindset and how self-talk affects you. There are two lists below: one characterizes the inner critic mindset, and the other list characterizes the inner coach mindset. Pay close attention, and notice the difference in how your body feels and your emotional response to the words of each of the thinking styles:

INNER CRITIC	VS.	INNER COACH
Weakness-Focus	⟷	Strengths-Focus
Problem-Oriented	⟷	Solution-Oriented
Fixed Mindset	⟷	Growth Mindset
Blame/Judge	⟷	Learn
Disregard	⟷	Respect
Know it Already	⟷	Curious
Afraid of Change	⟷	Open to Change
Either/Or Thinking	⟷	Creative Thinking
Use "But"	⟷	Use "And"
Looks for Offense	⟷	Looks for Intent

Inner Coach vs. Inner Critic Model, © 2014-2021,
Authentic Strengths Advantage, LLC. All rights reserved.

Did you notice any changes in how your body felt, or the thoughts or emotions you were having as you read each list? Which list had a more positive impact on you? Why? This simple activity evokes many insights for people. Without fail, people have reported discernable physical, mental, and emotional reactions, depending on the words they were reading. It's not surprising that positive psychology research is showing similar mind-body correlations to self-talk and thought patterns. Each of us engages in self-talk. We can choose to give voice to our inner critic or our inner coach. We will now explore the two mindsets...

Let's start with the inner critic. According to researcher Dr. Kristin Neff, self-criticism is a double-edged sword because when we engage in this mindset, we are both the attacker and the attacked. For example, musicians are notorious for being self-critical. Interestingly, a survey reported in an article in *The Music Quarterly*, musicians in 78 worldwide orchestras rated their job satisfaction lower than that of prison guards![16] Consider a top-performing concert musician who, in a quest for perfection, is painfully self-critical each time a mistake is made. Is that internal criticizing voice that I call the "inner critic," the key to the musician's success? Why do you think people are often self-critical?

Many people believe that self-criticism is necessary to motivate themselves. In fact, research is showing it's not a great motivator at all. Dr. Kristin Neff states, "Self-critics are much more likely to be anxious and depressed—not exactly get-up-and-go mindsets. They also have lower self-efficacy beliefs (i.e., self-confidence in their abilities), which undermines their potential for success. The habit of self-criticism engenders fear of failure, meaning that self-critics often don't even try achieving their goals because the possibility of failure is unacceptable. Even more problematic, self-critics have a hard time seeing themselves clearly and identifying needed areas of improvement because they know the self-punishment that will ensue if they admit the truth."[17]

Back to the two columns of words, the inner critic vs. the inner coach—the columns represent the inner mindset we have at any given time. We will stop throughout this book in each of the seven elements of well-being and do what I call a "mindset check" to determine which voice you are listening to—the inner critic or the inner coach. Checking your mindset is a powerful part of improving your well-being. The goal is to shift attention away from your inner critic and to listen more consistently to the empowering, positive, growth-inducing messages that come from your inner coach.

Take a moment to make a mark on each of the arrows where your mindset tends to be on this continuum. Notice if you currently lean more toward a coach or a critic mindset, and consider what you want to work on going forward. After you have marked the arrows, write down some strategies for moving to the inner coach side.

When we listen to our inner critic who undermines our values, attacks our self-worth, and blocks our initiative, we give away our stabilizing, self-motivating inner power. To identify the best path through life's distractions and the loud noise of the inner critic, we must acquire the skill of tuning into our inner coach instead.

One of my readers shared her experience using this tool: "Focusing on my character strengths has helped me to maneuver some difficult times in my life. This year, I started to go back to my old way of 'inner critic' thinking after being diagnosed with two autoimmune diseases. At first, I was upset about what I couldn't eat and my lack of energy. I was so focused on what was wrong with me instead of seeing what was strong. Even though I was keeping active, eating more mindfully, and creating healthier habits, I was struggling because my mindset wasn't in a positive place. After shifting my mindset to my 'inner coach,' my quality of life got better. I had less flare-ups and felt more at peace with my diagnosis. The mind is a powerful thing!"

Fortunately, we can retrain our thinking to listen to our inner coach and to notice our strengths so that we can appreciate the best in ourselves and in each moment. When we choose to listen to our inner coach, who expresses our personal vision and values, we inspire both ourselves and others to be more resourceful and creative. In these chapters, you will learn to give greater voice to your inner coach.

RECHARGE BY USING YOUR STRENGTHS

Most of us have experienced a time in life where we were burned out, stressed out, or stretched to our limits. These are typically times when our inner critic is in high gear. Let me share a true story about someone who was experiencing this: A woman who had recently been promoted sought strengths coaching because she was intimidated by the demands of her new job. Far from celebrating her success, her promotion was so stressful, she was nearly incapacitated by her fear of failure. She spent countless overtime hours working in a cluttered, drab workspace that she called "disheartening and overwhelming." She had stopped exercising to squeeze out more time from her hectic days, was living on unhealthy fast food, and had gained considerable weight. She experienced fitful sleep, was stressed about how to meet all the new demands, and her anxieties spilled over into her personal life. She found it impossible not to think about work during her personal time—frustrating her husband as well.

I encouraged this woman to spend time visualizing her ideal future and how her strengths would help her create this ideal future—in all aspects of her being. She identified the strengths she would call forth to recharge the essential elements of her life. She began listening to energizing music in the morning, placed fruit and healthful snacks within eyesight on her desk, took at least one movement break during the day, brought in some plants and re-positioned her desk so that she could see the greenery outside, and she turned off her work notifications on her phone after work hours to focus her attention on nurturing her personal life.

She regained her energy, and she was able to think more clearly once she could distinguish between the noise clamoring for her attention and the choices that aligned with her well-being goals. She learned to set boundaries by saying, "Let's schedule a time," so that she wasn't constantly interrupted from focused tasks. Her vision of her ideal future became her guide. She performed so well in her new job that she was promoted again.

This woman's example represents some of the processes you will go through to boost your own well-being. Write down your insights from her story in your *Well-Being Workbook*:

- What things did this woman do that you thought were "game changers" in improving her well-being—in regaining her energy and enthusiasm for the many areas of her life?
- Why do you think investing in those recharging activities not only made her feel better, but also improved her performance at work?

RECHARGE SEVEN ESSENTIAL ELEMENTS

Throughout this book, I've identified seven essential elements of well-being that, when recharged, can lead to sustainable energy, improve engagement, boost personal productivity, increase life satisfaction, and much more. As we learn about each of these seven essential elements in detail, we will identify specific ways to recharge each of them.

For example, we can recharge our mind through lifelong learning and acquiring new skills—education helps maintain mental focus and sharpness, as well as supports critical and creative thinking. The body has basic needs to function optimally: shelter, nutrition, rest, recovery time, etc. The healthier we are physically, the more engaged we will be and the better we will perform. The heart (a metaphor for our relationships with self and others) desires love, trust, healthy boundaries, forgiveness, and respect. The spirit is that part of us that hungers for meaning and purpose, a cause greater than self and the inward journey of self-discovery. As you read this book, I believe you will find a compelling case for recharging each of the seven essential elements of your well-being.

THE VALUE OF RECHARGING

So, what do I mean by "recharge"? In a *Harvard Business Review* article, "Resilience is About How You Recharge, Not How You Endure," Shawn Achor and Michelle Gielan asserted that taking the time to recharge is essential: "The key... is trying really hard, then stopping, recovering, and then trying again."[18] They offer compelling evidence for the benefits of recharging the important facets of ourselves. As parents of a young child, they describe their frenetic work life, coupled with the constant demands of parenthood, as a recipe for burnout. Unless, of course, one takes the time to recharge and recover. In their words: "Based on our current research, we have come to realize that the problem is not our hectic schedule...the problem comes from a misunderstanding of what it means to be resilient, and the resulting impact of overworking...We believe that the longer we tough it out, the tougher we are, and therefore the more successful we will be. However, this entire conception is scientifically inaccurate."[19]

But how do we care for the many aspects of our being? Jim Loehr and Tony Schwartz make a compelling case for recharging oneself in their book, *The Power of Full Engagement*: "To be fully engaged, we must be physically energized,

13

emotionally connected, mentally focused and spiritually aligned..."[20] When we recognize that recharging is vital to our overall well-being and success, we are more motivated and see it as a critical investment in ourselves, acknowledging that without stopping to recover, we lose the very ability to continue, or to contribute to others.

We all intuitively know that going full steam each day without recovery can backfire. According to Achor and Gielan, "You can start by strategically stopping. The very lack of a recovery period is dramatically holding back our collective ability to be resilient and successful. And lack of recovery—whether by disrupting sleep with thoughts of work or having continuous cognitive arousal by watching our phones—is costing our companies $62 billion a year (that's billion, not million) in lost productivity."[21] In other words, we need to stop and recharge the areas of our being that get depleted—investing in our well-being.

A great way to get motivated to recharge any of the seven elements is by enlisting your character strengths. When you leverage your strengths in activities that replenish these important aspects of yourself, you are more likely to follow through. For example, if you have a top strength of teamwork, your body recharging activity might be to enlist a friend to exercise with you. The more you connect your energizing top strengths to activities that recharge you, the more likely you will enjoy and continue the positive behaviors. As one person told me: "I've enjoyed writing down specific recharging activities involving each of my top strengths, then rotating through them to keep myself energized, positive, and focused on what's strong within."

ENERGY FLOW AND WELL-BEING

I have spent the last decade studying character strengths and their relationship to well-being. In recent years, additional research in fields such as biology, energy psychology, functional medicine, energy medicine, etc., has emerged about the relationship between energy flow and well-being. Luminaries like Bruce H. Lipton, PhD, world-renowned biologist and bestselling author of *The Biology of Belief*, have contributed to what we now know.

You could look at each of the seven elements of well-being in this book as "energy centers" that function best when they are recharged with positive, directed attention. Dr. Lipton explains why optimizing our energy is integral to our well-being: "A renaissance in cellular biology has recently revealed...thoughts and perceptions directly influence gene activity and cell behavior." He expounds: "The universe is one indivisible, dynamic whole in which energy and matter are so deeply entangled it's impossible to consider them as independent elements...to fully thrive, we must not only eliminate stressors, but also actively seek joyful, loving, fulfilling lives that stimulate growth..."[22] When I read Dr. Lipton's work, I noticed similarities between fortifying our inner coach with our character strengths and his advice for enhancing well-being by consciously directing our energy toward positive thoughts, feelings, and actions.

In fact, our thoughts and beliefs about ourselves and our surroundings (think inner coach vs. inner critic here) have a profound effect on our well-being. As Mark Hyman, MD, founder of the UltraWellness Center and Head of Strategy and Innovation at the Cleveland Clinic Center for Functional Medicine has said, "Thoughts are things. They can heal or harm. Beliefs mold your brain. This is not just a figurative metaphor for what happens. Your brain literally stiffens, slows and loses function in direct relationship to your [negative] thoughts, beliefs and attitudes about you and your place in the world. How each of us responds to our life—to our perceptions—has enormous implications for how we feel, how we age..."[23]

Michael Singer, author of the internationally acclaimed book, *The Untethered Soul*, also calls our awareness to the flow of our own energy: "It's actually a shame how little attention the Western world pays to the laws of inner energy. We study the energy outside, and give great value to energy resources, but we ignore the energy within...The truth is, every movement of your body, every emotion you have, and every thought that passes through your mind is an expenditure of energy."[24]

To summarize, each of us is a living embodiment of energy. The state of our energy affects the way we think, feel, and act. We constantly create reality with the energy we broadcast into the world when we approach life either positively or negatively (as a coach or as a critic). In turn, our energy is influenced by the people and situations we surround ourselves with. As we cultivate more empowering energy in our own lives by tapping into our character strengths, we also constructively impact the world around us. So, why not choose to be a positive contagion rather than a negative contagion? We can do this by leveraging our strengths and amplifying our inner coach. For example, why not use our time and energy to consciously build strengths, such as hope, love, and courage, as an antidote to the downward spiral of despair, anger, and fear?

I offer brief mindfulness practices to conclude each chapter in this book. Each mindfulness practice addresses the element of well-being that was discussed, corresponding with an energy center in the body where people tend to internalize that element. I call these "embodied mindfulness practices" for that reason. These practices provide an opportunity to quiet the mind so that you can go inward, listening to what your body and inner knowing are trying to tell you. The world's wisdom literature and ancient enduring philosophies have pointed to such energy centers for thousands of years, and to the value of recharging them. Now, well-being research and modern schools of thought are building upon this knowledge.[25] [26] [27] [28]

So, are you ready to dive into the first of the seven essential elements of well-being that we will explore together? As you turn the following pages, you will embark on an empowering journey to systematically recharge each element with your character strengths.

ENVIRONMENT

CHAPTER ONE

ENVIRONMENT

*"When a flower doesn't bloom,
you fix the environment in which it grows, not the flower."*[29]

—ALEXANDER DEN HEIJER

YOUR ENVIRONMENT

It's a basic truth that we are connected to our environment. We are in a dynamic relationship with our surroundings. Wherever we live and engage with others, our surroundings can affect us and vice versa. The good news is that we can positively influence our surroundings. With directed intention and action, we can create an environment that supports our authentic best selves.

The word "environment," in the context of well-being, refers to a person's sense of safety, rootedness, belonging, order, comfort, and how they relate to their world. Research about the mind-body connection has identified a clear relationship between our surroundings and our overall well-being. Studies show that our environment can:

- Influence mood
- Impact behavior and motivation
- Facilitate or discourage connection with others
- Create or reduce stress[30]

Studies also reveal that a healthy and pleasing environment does more than just improve your mood—it can actually affect a person's immune system and physical health.[31]

What do you think it means to create an environment that supports your authentic best self? This question helps us understand that there isn't one right way to create a positive and uplifting environment. Each person is unique and has different interests and likes—the key is to know what those are for you and implement them into your surroundings. A great way to create an environment that speaks to your authentic self is to tie it to your top character strengths.

For example, I coached a California woman who felt discouraged, anxious, and trapped in her home during COVID-19. To make matters worse, for a couple of weeks, she was unable to even venture into her back yard due to the smoke and ash from thousands of acres on fire in her state. She used her strengths of perseverance, hope, and love of learning to research air purifying house plants and mechanical air purifiers to create an oasis within her own home. She found comforting nature music soundtracks to play while she worked and watched enlivening nature films in the evenings to reconnect with the outdoors—even while sequestered. (Studies show that even short periods of time connecting with the outdoors can lift one's mood.) [32] This lifted her spirits during the most intense times of sheltering-in-place within her home. A silver lining from her time of trial is that it became a catalyst for her to participate in environmental causes, expanding her circle of influence.

Another example comes from Alex Stephany, whose actions demonstrate it's possible to creatively influence one's environment by helping others positively influence their own environments. He is the founder of Beam,[33] an online platform to crowdfund employment training for homeless people. It all began when Alex became friends with a homeless man sleeping outside his local transit station. He recognized that giving out the random warm drink or small handout wasn't bringing about significant change. He wanted to make a "real, tangible difference." Beam helps people who are homeless find work by connecting those in need with people wanting to train or hire them. Because of his creative solutions, Alex was chosen as one of several people making a positive difference by Eco-Age: "From building surveyors to beauticians, the platform breaks down the training each individual would need to get their ideal job."[34] He not only has impacted his environment around the transit station he regularly uses, but those he collaborates with have positively impacted their own environments as well. In

Alex's insightful words: "Sure, that's going to cost more than a cup of coffee...but what if we all chipped in?"[35]

ENVIRONMENT: CREATING A POSITIVE MINDSET

In this book, you will have the opportunity to perform what I call a "mindset check" customized for each of the seven elements of well-being. Each new mindset check will help you recognize which voice you are currently listening to most—the inner critic or the inner coach—for each specific element. Place a mark on the arrow continuum where you believe your mindset is currently. These mindset checks are also found in the *Well-Being Workbook*, or you can place a mark on this page. This will give you a visual to improve upon going forward.

INNER CRITIC	VS.	INNER COACH
Disconnected	←——→	Rooted/Belonging
Clutter/Chaos	←——→	Order/Clarity
Stressful/Anxious	←——→	Peaceful/Calm
Discomfort/Negativity	←——→	Comfort/Positivity
Unsettled/Unsafe	←——→	Refuge/Sanctuary
Uninviting	←——→	Inviting

Inner Coach vs. Inner Critic Model: Environment, © 2014-2021,
Authentic Strengths Advantage, LLC. All rights reserved.

Remember, research shows that our mindset is not fixed, but rather that it changes and evolves depending on where we focus our time and attention. This is often referred to as neuroplasticity, which means that we can literally reshape and retrain our brains. Therefore, the marks that you make on each of these arrows need not remain where they are. You can learn how to move those marks further toward the empowering inner coach spectrum. Developing an inner coach mindset is essential to recharging all aspects of our being.

ENVIRONMENT: THE CORE FOUR

Each of the seven elements contains what I call the "core four" principles for each element. We will discuss and define each principle as we explore ways to recharge that element to improve our whole life well-being. For the "environment" element in this book, these are the core four principles:

- **Rootedness/Belonging:** Our feelings of safety and security, physically or figuratively, grow when we feel rooted and a sense of belonging.
- **Refuge/Sanctuary:** Creating a place of refuge helps us feel secure.
- **Order/Cleanliness:** Bringing organization and cleanliness to one's environment increases well-being.
- **Positivity/Comfort:** Feeling supported by positive energy, positive emotions, and positive relationships is comforting.

Now, let's explore each of these core four principles one by one...

ROOTEDNESS AND BELONGING

The first core principle is "rootedness/belonging." Rootedness and belonging relate to our feelings of safety and security. Metaphorical rootedness and belonging can be more complex, yet is a deep human need. Dr. Kathryn Hall writes about belonging in *Psychology Today*, "Having a sense of belonging is a common experience. Belonging means acceptance as a member or part. Such a simple word for a huge concept. A sense of belonging is a human need, just like the need for food and shelter. Feeling that you belong is most important in seeing value in life and in coping with intensely painful emotions."[36]

Kevin Hearne, an urban fantasy novelist, described the feeling of rootedness in a beautiful, poetic way. He said "I forgot how good it feels to be rooted. And to be rooted is not the same thing at all as being tied down. To be rooted is to say, here I am nourished and here will I grow, for I have found a place where every sunrise shows me how to be more than what I was yesterday, and I need not wander to feel the wonder of my blessing. And when you are rooted, defending that space ceases to be an obligation or a duty and becomes more of a desire."[37]

REFUGE AND SANCTUARY

The next core principle of environment is "refuge/sanctuary." The Oxford definition of refuge is "a condition of being safe or sheltered from pursuit, danger, or trouble."[38]

Let's first talk about taking refuge. Meditation master, Yongey Mingyur Rinpoche, writes: "Everyone takes refuge in something. Often, it's in relationships, locations, or activities that offer the body or mind a sense of security and protection."[39]

We can ask ourselves these questions: Where do we look for our own happiness? How do we create conditions that support our own comfort or security? It's important that we seek refuge through conditions that are good for us—through healthy behaviors, positive relationships, and activities that help us grow and thrive.

While refuge is identified as a *condition* of safety, sanctuary is defined as a *place* of safety.[40] Let me share a story of someone who created her own personal sanctuary with a tremendous positive outcome.

A blogger named Lisa shares a story about her sixteen-year-old daughter, who after several years of behavioral and health challenges, was facing termination from her special needs school and being recommended for a residential treatment center—or institutionalization. At the same time, Lisa's marriage was unraveling, her business was becoming overwhelming, and the combination of these issues brought her life to an abrupt halt. Lisa writes: "And it was around that time that there was a morning that I remember so clearly. I was walking our dogs early and had just rounded the corner to see the sunrise beginning to glow. A breeze swirled around me and lifted my hair, and the word 'sanctuary' whispered in my mind. It captivated my imagination and I found myself wondering what this luminous word could mean to my life and to my business."

As an interior designer, Lisa began to envision how she could create a sanctuary space for her daughter and for herself. Lisa's focus was to create an environment that would "nurture and support not only our bodies, but our spirits as well." Lisa concludes: "an amazing thing happened: as I created peace around me, I found it inspired peace within me. I realized then that sanctuary was not only a tool to survive, but to thrive. [My daughter's] sanctuary gave her a place to process her own experiences and emotions, regroup, and present to the world the very best version of herself. And my sanctuary gave me the chance to do the same."[41]

Refuge and safety are words that apply to our own homes and workplaces, but those words also apply to the greater home we all live in—planet earth. Christopher Barrington-Leigh, an assistant professor at McGill University, writes: "As we seek to create environments of refuge and safety within our own homes and workplaces, it's important that we also look to the grand home we all share—the planet earth." He goes on to say: "Converging bodies of research indicate that well-being and ecological sustainability, goals sometimes viewed as contradictory, are in fact complementary. Emphasizing social drivers of well-being counters the conventional focus on economic growth and fosters the pro-social attitudes and behaviors necessary to live in better balance with nature. Fortuitously, recent technological innovations that make knowledge and productive capacity widely available at little cost and promote creative and collaborative activity could facilitate a transition to a world of reduced environmental stress and enhanced human well-being."[42]

ORDER AND CLEANLINESS

The third core foundational principle is "order/cleanliness." Scientists now assert that keeping things clean and organized is good for your well-being. Here's what the research says:

- Clean spaces promote health and physical activity.
- Home cleanliness is a greater predictor of physical health than neighborhood walkability.
- Cluttered spaces can correlate with higher levels of the stress hormone cortisol.
- Decluttered spaces increase focus on tasks. This is due to the visual cortex becoming overwhelmed by task-irrelevant objects, making it harder to allocate attention and complete tasks efficiently.
- Making your bed each morning can promote healthy rest. People who were surveyed also reported benefits from having clean sheets—specifically, 75 percent of people said they get a better night's rest with clean sheets because they feel more comfortable.[43]

These statistics are not designed to make people feel guilty or ashamed about things being messy. Rather, the purpose of highlighting this research is to recognize the incredible benefits that can come from creating more order in one's environment. Meagan Francis, founder of the website *Life, Listened* states: "Cleaning and organizing is a practice, not a project. It's never too late to begin developing the practice of bringing more order into one's environment."[44] Each of us can choose to implement this practice at any point.

One of my colleagues, after struggling with a serious health issue, shared the following: "I challenged myself to make my bed for 30 days about a year ago. It was amazing to see how much more productive and excited for life I was after those 30 days. I did it during a time when it was hard for me to even get out of bed. I decided that if I didn't get anything else done that day, I could feel good about making my bed. My mindset improved over time because I could see at least one task accomplished every single day. The small achievement of making my bed evolved into completing lots of other tasks and moving towards a thriving state of living, beyond just surviving."

The list below is adapted from research conducted by the University of Minnesota. Your spaces, at home and at work, can do the following:

- **Impact Mood:** Research studies show that brightly lit spaces can positively impact depression and anxiety.
- **Increase Motivation:** When a space is already clean, it may motivate you to put things away.
- **Encourage Interactions:** A warm and welcoming space produces comfort and is conducive for people to gather and positively interact.
- **Raise/Lower Stress Levels:** Environments ultimately affect all elements of a person's whole life well-being.[45]

COMFORT AND POSITIVITY

The fourth and final core principle of environment is "comfort/positivity." Distinguished positive psychology researcher Dr. Barbara Fredrickson has identified "contentment" as one of the four basic positive human emotions. When a person experiences comfort in their environment, which is closely connected with contentment, it's likely that this person is experiencing positive emotions, or positivity.[46]

How, then, can one create "comfort?" The word "comfort" is used as a noun, verb, and an adjective. When used as a noun, one definition is "a state of physical ease." As a verb, one definition is: "to make someone feel less unhappy." It can be used as an adjective when describing a person's favorite food, as "comfort food."[47]

Let's now look at a principle of positivity: positivity begets more positivity. In fact, research shows that positivity is contagious.[48] When you are positive with another person, he or she is more likely to return the favor. Appreciating others creates an upward spiral of positivity and leads to optimal experiences. There are myriad benefits to positivity—dozens of global studies have shown that when people are exposed to positivity, they see more solutions in puzzles, score higher on cognitive tasks, remember more information, and have stronger relationships.[49] So, the key is to become the catalyst that puts the upward spiral into action. As Dr. Tal Ben-Shahar sums it up: "When you appreciate the good, the good appreciates."[50] Achieving an appreciative atmosphere in our lives and our relationships requires looking for what's going well—again, changing our perspective from "what's wrong" to "what's strong"—catching the positives as they occur and not letting them slip by without acknowledgement.

In addition, positive emotions are linked with better health, a longer life, and greater well-being. On the other hand, chronic anger, worry, and hostility increase the risk of various diseases.

For some people, creating a happy environment comes naturally and easily. Others need to work at it. How does one go about becoming happier? That's where positive psychology comes in. This exciting new science has been exploring how people and organizations can support the quest for increased satisfaction and meaning. According to a Harvard Medical School blog, positive psychology has uncovered several routes to happiness, which I believe also contribute to a positive environment, as follows:

- **Feeling Good:** seeking pleasurable emotions and sensations
- **Engaging Fully:** pursuing goals and activities that engage you fully
- **Doing Good:** searching for meaning outside yourself
- **Expressing Gratitude:** expressing appreciation for what you have in your life
- **Savoring Pleasure:** placing your attention on pleasure as it occurs and consciously enjoying the experience as it unfolds

- **Being Mindful:** focusing your attention on what is happening at the moment and accepting it without judgment
- **Self-Compassion:** consoling yourself as needed, taking the time to nurture yourself, and building the motivation to try again[51]

RECHARGE YOUR ENVIRONMENT WITH STRENGTHS

One of the most powerful ways we can recharge each element is by connecting activities to our character strengths. This practice yields positive outcomes.

We discussed at the beginning of this book the tremendous benefits that come from engaging in and expressing our character strengths. Among many positive outcomes are the recharging of the elements of whole life well-being. This leads to sustainable energy, engagement, increased personal productivity, and an overall sense of improved well-being, just to name a few.

You can increase your motivation to recharge each of the seven elements of well-being by enlisting your strengths in activities that replenish these important aspects of yourself. There are countless ways we can use our character strengths to recharge any of the elements of whole life well-being. To jumpstart your thinking, I will provide a few examples of how you might recharge each particular element. You are also encouraged to come up with your own activities that are connected to things you enjoy doing, or to your top character strengths.

Here are just three examples to generate ideas of how you can use your character strengths to recharge your environment. Of course, you may want to use other character strengths of your choosing.

HUMOR	CREATIVITY	BRAVERY
Infuse humor in self-talk or with others to bring positive energy to your environment.	Redesign and de-clutter a space in your home or workplace to be more functional and inviting.	Make needed changes to your environment to feel more secure, peaceful, and grounded. Protect your refuge.

EXERCISE: BEST SELF

What if each of us could recreate a past best self experience at will—how would that benefit us? How can we intentionally call upon our strengths best suited to any task to help us perform at our best? We are now going to do a fun exercise called "Best Self" and apply it to this particular environment element. Think of a time when you contributed to or created a positive environment that benefited you and/or others. A time when you felt really great about something you accomplished as it relates to one or all of the core four principles of this environment element. In your *Well-Being Workbook*, write your answers to the following questions:

- What did you do to make this happen? Describe your environment during this successful experience. Did you feel a sense of belonging? Was there positivity in your environment?
- In what ways were your strengths best used in past successes in creating a positive environment? How could your strengths be applied today, and in the future, to make your environment more beneficial to you?
- Why are some of your top strengths not being employed currently, and how could these strengths be brought forward more consistently?
- What elements of your best self experience could be re-created to achieve more success in creating a positive environment for you going forward?

ENVIRONMENT: MINDFULNESS PRACTICE

Let's conclude our exploration of the environment element with a mindfulness practice. *Wikipedia* defines a mindfulness practice as: "a way of paying attention...in a particular way: on purpose, in the present moment, and non-judgmentally...Bringing one's complete attention to the present experience on a moment-to-moment basis."[52]

The mindfulness practice you are about to do is an embodied mindfulness practice because it reconnects you with your body and your energy centers, deepening what you have learned in this chapter. So, what is "embodied positive psychology"? It's developing your awareness of what is happening in your body, related to your life experiences and your resulting reactions, in order to improve your well-being. As Megan McDonough, CEO of the Whole Being Institute, defines embodied positive psychology: "Embodied positive psychology engages the body in the kinesthetic experience of living the science of flourishing."

McDonough goes on to explain: "Cognitive understanding and knowing is not the same as realizing, living, and experiencing. Embodiment physicalizes an idea, making it concrete in the here and now. As the definition explains, embodiment gives visible form to an idea. By embodying positive psychology, you become a walking expression of the idea. Embodied positive psychology is the experience of:

- Cultivating mindfulness through the body, by focusing on the breath and anchoring our attention in the present
- Engaging the body as part of the learning process—physically moving in order to understand an intellectual concept
- Exploring and inquiring as much about our inner world as our outer world
- Sharing, connecting, and networking, because the 'we' helps provide context for the 'me'
- Leveraging the body's capacity to change the mind (instead of enforcing the mind's will upon the body)"[53]

McDonough asserts: "Philosophers, psychologists, and even artificial-intelligence researchers who study the embodied mind contend that the body shapes cognition. Or, to put it more simply, the body shapes what we think and how we feel—and, by extension, how we act."[54]

So, are you ready to experience an embodied mindfulness practice to recharge your environment? Find a comfortable place where you will not be disturbed. Take time to be still as you check in with this energy center in your body and listen to the inner wisdom that surfaces for you during this practice. Perhaps you will notice an increased motivation to make positive changes, or an elevated sense of energy and ease. You can choose to mindfully read and reflect on the written mindfulness practice below, or you can listen to the mindfulness practices online at AuthenticStrengths.com.

Place your awareness on the base of your spine,
extending through your legs where you are grounded.
Now imagine that this corresponds to your sense of rootedness
within your environment, to survival and safety.
Envision a physical space or refuge for yourself that is orderly,
comfortable, positive, and secure.
Recharge by saying: I am rooted, safe, and I focus on the positive.
Take a moment to experience and linger
in the positive emotions this evokes for you.

ABUNDANCE

CHAPTER TWO

ABUNDANCE

"Abundance is not something we acquire. It's something we tune into."[55]

—DR. WAYNE DYER

YOUR SENSE OF ABUNDANCE

Now let's launch into the next element: abundance. While exploring this element, we will take a closer look at what it means to experience abundance in life.

But first, let's look at what gets in the way of experiencing a sense of abundance. Our world can appear steeped in a scarcity mentality. We are inundated daily with disturbing news headlines, and with unrealistic social media pressures to portray a perfect life as we are lured to compare ourselves to others. We may carry a deficit perspective of ourselves and of others. As a result, we may not be aware of how it affects our own sense of abundance, our well-being, and the vibrancy of our relationships in our personal lives, at school, at work, in our communities, and so on.[56]

Too often, we view abundance as things outside of us that we need to acquire. This view of abundance keeps us focusing on what we don't yet have—what we have yet to acquire—leading us to the scarcity mentality mentioned previously.

Further, people mistakenly equate abundance with financial wealth and the things we can buy with that wealth. In fact, abundance is a much greater principle than that—far beyond anything a person could ever hope to own.

So then, what is abundance? Abundance is a universal principle that states that you already are abundant with talents, strengths, and potential. You already are creative, resourceful, and whole, and the key is to understand how to access this potential. Seeing abundance in this way—as intrinsic potential—opens us to unlimited possibilities!

The late Dr. Wayne Dyer confirms this greater, more expansive view of abundance as being something "we tune into."[57] While it may seem difficult to believe, especially when life is challenging, in reality, we already have everything we need to live an abundant life. As the quote in this chapter heading says, the most important ingredient for abundance is attitude, and your attitude is something you can influence.

During this chapter, we will learn how to develop, or tune into, abundance in your present life, independent of circumstances, situations, or things. Webster's dictionary defines abundance as "an ample quantity" and the related word "prosperity" as: "a successful, flourishing, or thriving condition."[58]

People often associate the words "abundance" and "prosperity" as the accumulation of money and financial wealth. Though these words can, in part, be associated with money and financial wealth, some people may have a negative view of these words when they *only* attach them to money. In fact, abundance and prosperity are so much more than that. Prosperity, like the term abundance, can be an attitude toward life, or a mindset. We can choose to have an abundant or prosperous mind. The irony is that an abundant and prosperous mind may often actually help us experience better financial health. The following family example was sent to me via email:

> Our family has focused on abundance during the pandemic. There were definitely trial periods, like when our kids got sent home from school and I became a homeschool mom of 4 overnight! It was overwhelming at first and took work and organization.
>
> Over time, my husband and I tapped into our strengths and worked on creating strong mindsets. We thought that things would fall apart with the unprecedented changes of the pandemic, but things actually became better for our family than they had been in a long time. Our family became stronger and closer. My husband was resourceful with his business and was able

to find work through a time that was stressful and challenging. I found peace and joy in having my kids home, teaching and learning alongside them. My husband and I worked more as a team than ever before. I discovered that by taking on the challenge of the pandemic, our family shifted into resilience mode, making the best of what we could. We were able to cultivate happiness in simple things. We felt like the richest people in the world with good health, a roof over our heads, food in our bellies, and being together. Money became a means for us, not a focus of worth or something with which we compared ourselves to others. Our finances have followed suit, surprisingly becoming better than they have been in a long time.

There are many reasons people experience financial struggles and sometimes there aren't immediate solutions within our grasp. One strategy that has shown a positive impact is to focus on the good. A 2019 research study, highlighted in a *Harvard Business Review* article, "The Financial Upside of Being an Optimist" by Michelle Gielan, found that optimists experience much fewer days of stress each year than pessimists. Gielan summarized: "an antidote to chronic stress is cultivating an optimistic mindset...We surveyed more than 2,000 Americans...the data clearly showed that optimists were significantly more likely to experience better financial health than pessimists and engage in healthier habits with their money...the most compelling finding was how optimists felt, reporting that they stressed about finances 145 fewer days each year as compared to pessimists...Optimism is a lucrative investment beyond one's finances." [59]

Hope and optimism, it seems, can be a wise investment for both your well-being—and your abundance. But how does one develop such positive emotions to increase one's abundance? The key is to regularly check in with your mindset and to continually work to shift it toward gratitude for what you already have. From there you have more energy to create even greater abundance in your life.

ABUNDANCE: CREATING A POSITIVE MINDSET

Let's check in with our mindset—this time regarding how we view abundance. The inner critic tries to challenge an abundance mindset by keeping us mired in scarcity, envy, perfectionism, obsessive competition, and fear of failure. By listening to our inner coach, we can reject scarcity and the focus on never having enough. We can choose to see ourselves and others as full of infinite potential, leading to self-compassion, acceptance, and gratitude rather than criticism, lack, and shame.

Again, place a mark where you are currently on the arrow continuum for each statement about the abundance mindset. Remember, you can work on these areas and move toward the coach end of the spectrum over time.

INNER CRITIC	VS.	INNER COACH
Scarcity-Focus	⟷	Abundance-Focus
Individualistic	⟷	Team-Oriented
Comparison-Focus	⟷	Enough/Plenty
Adrift/Directionless	⟷	Future Plan
Defensive/Threatened	⟷	Solution-Oriented
Afraid of Change	⟷	Seek Common Ground

Inner Coach vs. Inner Critic Model: Abundance, ©2014-2021,
Authentic Strengths Advantage, LLC. All rights reserved.

Notice that the inner critic/inner coach statements are examples of self-talk. Those who focus on listening to the inner coach understand the importance of using creative, solution-oriented, and encouraging language. When we use negative, blaming, or self-deprecating language, in essence, we're saying that we're victims—that we do not influence our own destiny. When we obsessively think about all the things causing us stress, we override our creative options to influence our situation. Consequently, we have less time and energy to spend on the very things that will change our situation for the better. Even if your creative bandwidth appears small, I encourage you to stay focused on it. What you focus on grows, and little by little, it will expand. You will surprise yourself with your increased options.

Tony Robbins once stated: "When you are grateful, fear disappears and abundance appears."[60] Gratitude is one of the most powerful ways we can learn to have an abundance mindset. Research overwhelmingly shows that people who practice gratitude consistently report a host of physical, mental and social benefits.[61] For example, people who write a gratitude list each day report higher levels of happiness and life satisfaction. A great time to do this is first thing in the morning or before going to sleep at night. Another option is to mentally list what you are grateful for when you are faced with the temptation to compare yourself to others.

Let me share the rest of the email I received from the family previously mentioned, as each member of their family worked to expand their strength of gratitude: "We did this as a family this year. We would share in the morning two things that we were grateful for. If my husband had already headed off to work when the kids and I woke up, we would call him and report it before school. At first, it took our kids a while to think of things to say. But after a week or two, they would spout off a list of things they were grateful for. Our mornings seemed to go smoother with this practice. There was less bickering. Instead of feelings of frustration or discord in the morning, there was a feeling of peace, teamwork, and optimism. It really didn't take long to do the gratitude practice and became something fun for us to look forward to each morning."

Below is a profound quote about gratitude from the makers of the film series, *Gratitude Revealed* by Louie Schwarzberg: "Practicing gratitude does not ignore the harsh realities of life; in fact, it accepts them, then encourages us to identify some amount of goodness in our life. Looking a little deeper into where this sense of goodness comes from, we can see that much of this appreciation stems from external sources. Gratitude can humble us and help us acknowledge that other people—or even higher powers, if you're of a spiritual mindset, gave us many gifts, big and small, to help us achieve the goodness in our lives."[62]

ABUNDANCE: THE CORE FOUR

As I mentioned in the previous chapter, each element contains core principles I call the "core four." Let's take a look at the core four principles of abundance. They are:

- **Resourcefulness/Creativity:** We each have potential within to create the abundance and prosperity we desire.
- **Future Plan:** Preparation and providing for our future needs is wise.
- **Savor:** Being fully present with all five senses to enjoy each moment is essential to the experience of abundance.
- **Enough/Plenty:** Living abundantly also involves an affirming attitude that "I am enough, and I have enough," but doesn't preclude one from further accomplishments.

Let's dive into the core four principles of abundance, starting with re-sourcefulness/creativity...

RESOURCEFULNESS AND CREATIVITY

So, how can you use your resourcefulness and creativity to increase your abundance? Lexico defines "resourceful" as: "Having the ability to find quick and clever ways to overcome difficulties."[63] And "creativity" is defined by Webster's as "the ability or power to create."[64] We can envision being a resourceful or creative problem-solver, using our resourcefulness to create abundance and prosperity in our lives. Therefore, if you combine your "resourcefulness" and "creativity," you acknowledge your ability or potential to influence your own abundance.

I remember the time I was invited to teach refugees and aid workers in Malawi, Africa with the International Rescue Committee. I did a creativity exercise with this group that I had done countless times before in my workshops with diverse cultures around the world, but this time I was surprised with the results. I asked the participants to look at a paper cup placed in front of them, and to work with one other person to identify as many creative uses as possible for that paper cup that they could think of. Then I timed them for 90 seconds.

I was amazed to witness an explosion of resourceful uses for the paper cup that I had never witnessed to such an extent elsewhere, after decades of doing this exercise. Each person who participated in the exercise literally came alive with energy! They examined the cup from all possible angles, looking at how it diffused light by holding it up to a light bulb, throwing the cup in the air or rolling it to carefully observe its movement qualities, attaching it to other items in the room, drawing on it, cutting it up and creatively using its parts for dozens of surprising purposes, and even placing the cup on their heads, or using it as an article of clothing, etc. This group doubled the highest number of creative uses I had ever observed in any other country!

At the conclusion of the exercise, the entire group reflected on what they had just experienced. They explained that when given the opportunity, resources, or tools, they were eager and passionate to improve the quality of their lives—leveraging their resourcefulness and creativity. One person then showed me how people in their community would repurpose a used plastic liter soda bottle into sandals by cutting holes into the halved soda bottles and threading rope through the holes to attach the sandals to their feet. Another person shared how he had collected rubber bands and discarded pieces of cloth, then carefully fashioned them into a functional soccer ball by tightly wrapping the cloth and binding it neatly with the rubber bands. Because they had very little, they literally lived from a place of heightened awareness and gratitude for all that they had, opening up a plethora of possibilities.

What if we followed their lead—opening our perspective to see our own situations with fresh eyes so that we can create the abundance we desire in our lives? We might be surprised to notice resources and strengths we hadn't noticed before. The solutions to our abundance issues could be hiding in plain view if we could only shift our awareness.

Back here in the U.S., one person who had read about the experience I had in Africa emailed me about the liberating act of donating many boxes of excessive belongings, which resulted in a wonderful feeling of abundance, freedom, and purpose—finding more time and energy to focus on the important things in life, rather than "feeling like a servant caring for so much stuff." As the great Greek philosopher, Epicurus, stated, "Not what we have, but what we enjoy, constitutes our abundance."[65]

FUTURE PLAN

Let's turn to the next core principle, "future plan," and why it's important to begin working on it now. Poet and lecturer David Whyte, while conducting a workshop for AT&T employees about giving up "personal vision" and "sacred desires" to profit a company, had a memorable experience. Reportedly, a woman in his workshop wrote a poem with the following words: "Ten years ago...I turned my face for a moment...and it became my life."[66] In essence, this woman was describing living her life unconsciously—just going through the motions—without any form of a constructive, conscious future plan. This poem strikes a familiar chord with people who have put their dreams on hold. For example, how many people show up for work just to watch the clock until quitting time and only come alive on the weekends when work is over?

Why do we postpone our plans and even our joy? "I'll be happy when..." or "If only..." are common ways we do this. We sometimes look away at momentary distractions or settle for immediate, but empty, gratification as the years fly by. What if we turned our faces toward our vision, dreams, and plans, while savoring the present? Only when we are authentic with ourselves can we make this exploration. And when we connect with our authentic selves, we harness the power of living in the now, mindfully present—while creating an even brighter future.

When you practice self-care, plan for a better future, and follow up on your commitments to yourself, others benefit as well. You can make your best contributions to others by bringing your whole self to all aspects of living—your work and personal life are parts of the same, sacred, whole person that you are.

EXERCISE: ENJOY THE NOW, CREATE THE FUTURE

It's possible to bring our plans to reality by creating a clear mental picture of ourselves successfully using our character strengths to realize our dreams. This power of visualization has been shown to be effective for decades—people use visualization techniques around the world—from athletes, to teachers, to emergency personnel, to executives. Answer these questions in your *Well-Being Workbook*:

- Are you postponing joy? If so, how are you delaying the little, simple moments of feeling happy and satisfied with life each day?
- What "perfect" conditions are you waiting for to pursue your dreams?
- What can you create in the here and now that brings you joy?
- What steps, even if small, can you take now to contribute to your ideal future plan?
- Visualize your ideal future filled with abundance. What do you see and experience as you visualize this scene and imagine yourself in it?

SAVOR THE GOOD

The next core principle of abundance is "savor." The definition of savoring from *Wikipedia* is "the use of thoughts and actions to increase the intensity, duration, and appreciation of positive experiences and emotions...Positive psychology uses the concept of savoring as a way to maximize the potential benefits that positive experiences and emotions can have on peoples' lives."[67]

Psychologist Tchiki Davis defines it this way: "Savoring just means that we attempt to fully feel, enjoy, and extend our positive experiences. Savoring is a great way to develop a long-lasting stream of positive thoughts and emotions, because positive events cannot always be relied on to make you happier."[68]

According to Dr. Fred Bryant, there are four dimensions of savoring. They are:

- **Marveling**: losing ourselves in awe and wonder
- **Luxuriating**: indulging our senses, like we do when we bite into rich and delicious chocolate
- **Basking**: focusing on receiving praise
- **Thanksgiving**: expressing gratitude[69]

We can learn to savor in all four of these dimensions. We will get an opportunity to practice savoring at the end of this section. Most people are primed to experience pleasure in special moments, like a wedding or a vacation. Everyday pleasures, on the other hand, can slip by without much notice. Savoring means placing your attention on pleasure as it occurs, consciously enjoying the experience as it unfolds. Appreciating the treasures in life, big and small, helps build happiness.

Lastly, it's important to consider that multitasking is an enemy of savoring. Try as you might, you can't fully pay attention to multiple things. If you're scanning the newspaper and listening to the radio during breakfast, you're not getting the pleasure you could from that meal—or the newspaper or radio program. If you're walking the dog on a beautiful path but mentally staring at your day's to-do list, you're missing the moment. Research has shown that multitasking doesn't actually put us ahead. As the Cleveland Clinic has recently asserted, "the science is clear—multitasking doesn't work."[70] Why? Because it impairs your best thinking and divides your attention.

HAVING ENOUGH

The final principle of the abundance element is "enough/plenty." As my mentor, Dr. Stephen R. Covey, once said, "The more we develop an abundance mentality, the more we are genuinely happy for the success, well-being, recognition and good fortune of other people. We believe their success adds to, rather than detracts, from our lives."[71] We can each get caught up in comparison—the opposite of enough and plenty—by comparing what we have to what others have, thus feeling a lack or having a scarcity mindset. This type of excessive comparing is a non-productive perception that can color everything in our world. Mark Twain once said, "Comparison is the death of joy."[72] All people compare. For example, people compare athletic ability, financial status, possessions, looks, etc.

When comparison turns from perceptive discernments to discriminating judgments that rank things, it becomes a fear-based pursuit that separates people into categories rather than uniting them. When we look for what makes us better or worse than someone else instead of looking for uniting factors, such as what we can learn from another person, we contribute to the illusion that we are more different than alike.

With this kind of thinking, we reaffirm the fallacy that human worth can be distilled into comparisons. Ultimately, "comparanoia," a trendy, made-up word that means excessive comparing, is destructive in its consequences. Someone must be better because they have more or "are" more; and someone must be worse because they have less or what they do or are is perceived as "less than."

Comparing our own progress or success with others' successes has been characterized as "keeping up with the Joneses," based on a comic strip that originated in the U.S. in the early 1900s. In it, a never-seen neighboring family was portrayed as having a bigger house, greener lawn, better furnishings, more success at work, nicer children, and an enviable relationship.[73]

Today, instead of comic strips, we have social media. Every culture has its own version of social envy, and social media now plays a large part in trapping people into striving for things they don't really need, but think they want because those things are perceived as status symbols. There is a manipulative component in social media that, left unchecked, competes for our own sense of autonomy. Even worse, a growing obsession with how many "likes" we get on Instagram, Facebook, or Twitter derides our sense of self-worth in a subtle, yet corrosive way.[74]

In her book, *The Future of Happiness*, author Amy Blankson offers insights, "Technology, at least in theory, is improving our productivity, efficiency, and communication. The one thing it's not doing is making us happier... knowing that technology is here to stay and will continue to evolve in form and function, we need to know how to navigate the future to achieve a better balance between technology, productivity, and well-being... By rethinking when, where, why, and how you use technology, you will not only influence your own well-being but also help shape the future of your community."[75]

Now that we have an increased awareness of "comparanoia" and its role in social media, let's shift our attention to how we can cultivate more positive emotions—such as cultivating an empowering sense of enough and plenty.

RECHARGE YOUR ABUNDANCE WITH STRENGTHS

To help jump-start your thinking, here are three examples of how to recharge the element of abundance, using your character strengths. You can use any of your character strengths that most resonate with you to invigorate this element of abundance.

PRUDENCE	HONESTY	GRATITUDE
Plan for the future by opening or adding to a savings plan.	Conduct an honest assessment of your finances. Make changes where needed.	List five things you are grateful for. Do this morning and night to strengthen your abundance mindset.

EXERCISES: SAVORING

We are going to do two short exercises to help us recharge the element of abundance—specifically by practicing savoring. Let's start by practicing being fully present in the use of our five senses. This exercise is sometimes used to combat the anxiety that comes with feeling fear or scarcity. Write your answers to the following prompts in your *Well-Being Workbook*:

- Acknowledge **FIVE** things you see around you. It could be a pen, a spot on the ceiling, anything in your surroundings.
- Acknowledge **FOUR** things you can touch around you.
- Acknowledge **THREE** things you can hear.
- Acknowledge **TWO** things you can smell.
- Acknowledge **ONE** thing you can taste.[76]

Another exercise that can increase your sense of abundance is the following "savoring" activity. Simply spend ten minutes writing about a happy, joyful, or pleasant event that happened earlier this week. For example, you could write about a good conversation you had with a friend.

- Recall the people, smells, sounds, physical sensations, and sights that you experienced at the time of the event.
- Focus on the positive emotions that you felt during and right after this event.
- Focus on how this positive event occurred and how you created this situation for yourself.[77]

ABUNDANCE: MINDFULNESS PRACTICE

Let's conclude our exploration of abundance with a mindfulness practice to improve your sense of abundance in your life.

Find a comfortable place where you will not be disturbed. Mindfully read, experience, and reflect on this written mindfulness practice below, or you can listen to the mindfulness practices at <u>AuthenticStrengths.com</u>:

Move your attention to the area below your navel.
Imagine this corresponds with your sense of abundance,
your creativity and savoring with your five senses.
Envision a future in which you experience plenty in all areas of your life,
where your good intentions and wishes are fulfilled, blessing yourself and others.
Recharge as you say: I am abundant, creative, resourceful and whole.
Take a moment to savor the positive emotions this has induced for you.

BODY

CHAPTER THREE

BODY

"Embrace and love your body. It's the most amazing thing you'll ever own."

—ANONYMOUS

YOUR BODY

Let's move to the next element of whole life well-being: the body. Remember, to function optimally, our body has basic needs that must be met: shelter, nutrition, rest, recovery time, etc. [78] The healthier you are physically, the more engaged you will likely be and the better you will perform. [79] This doesn't just help *you*—it's also essential for your ability to contribute to *others*, similar to the well-known instructions every airline gives to those on board before take-off: "Put the oxygen mask on yourself first." Some of us may be dealing with health challenges, and in the midst of such hardships, we often develop an awareness of how to nurture and value our bodies like never before, inspiring others to do so as well.

Mahatma Gandhi also asserted the importance of taking care of our body: "It is health that is the real wealth, and not pieces of gold and silver." [80] In addition, the Buddha is attributed as saying: "To keep the body in good health is a duty—otherwise we shall not be able to keep our mind strong and clear." [81] Furthermore, there is little question that the mind influences the body and vice-versa. Dr. Andrew Steptoe of University College London probed the biological connection between happiness and health in a study published in the *American Journal of Epidemiology*. The study showed that positive emotions are connected with biological responses that are "health-protective." [82]

Another study of 193 healthy volunteers by Carnegie Mellon University provided evidence that happiness can strengthen the immune system, according to Dr. Sheldon Cohen. After exposure to cold viruses, volunteers with high levels of positive emotions were more resistant to disease.[83] The book, *Relaxation Revolution*, by Herbert Benson, MD, and William Proctor, JD, notes the power our mindset can have on our bodies: "Gradually, study after mind body study, carried out with the most careful scientific protocols, produced incontrovertible evidence that the mind can indeed influence—and heal—the body."[84] A health and wellness coach who has read my books, sent me the following personal example:

> I interact with many people who are in different stages of their health journey. Those that tend to experience consistent good health seem to be healthy in the mind as well as the body. They don't ignore one or the other, combining the two synergistically. My body and mind haven't always been on the same level of healthy and I had an illuminating experience after working hard on my own health journey. I was at my peak physically, while I overlooked my mental health needs. Over the span of six months, my physical health began to decline as well. I went from doing intense workouts seven days a week, to barely being able to get out of bed. I eventually couldn't do even ten-minute workouts. I had no appetite. My adrenals were shot, I had Epstein-Barr Virus, and my muscles were deteriorating. It was one of the hardest things I have experienced. I had to learn to slow down and be honest about my mental health. My physical health didn't last in spite of the hard work and restrictive diet. I wasn't really happy, and my body followed suit when my mind wasn't on board.

BODY: CREATING A POSITIVE MINDSET

Before we dive into the core four principles of the body, we will revisit the value of a mindset check. Remember that our mindset affects our body, and vice versa. Developing an awareness of our mindset is an important first step in improving our well-being.

Back to the health and wellness coach who shared her personal story previously, she goes on to share: "Just as my unhealthy mind had a negative effect on my physical health, strengthening my mind has been the key thing in helping my physical health become better. I now incorporate meditation, affirmations, and other mental exercises in my daily routine. Without a healthy mind, I find that my physical health doesn't last long."

Take a moment to conduct a mindset check about the body element. Place a mark where you are currently on the arrow continuum for each statement. Where would you like to be over time?

INNER CRITIC	VS.	INNER COACH
Overwhelmed	←——→	Focused
Shame/Demean Body	←——→	Love/Honor Body
Food = Enemy	←——→	Food = Nourishment
Conditional Worth	←——→	Innate Worth
Judge/Condemn	←——→	Forgive/Accept

Inner Coach vs. Inner Critic Model: Body, © 2014-2021,
Authentic Strengths Advantage, LLC. All rights reserved.

BODY: CORE FOUR

Below are the core four principles of the body:

- **Nutrition/Fitness:** Recharging the body through exercise and nutrition is one of the most powerful ways to enhance well-being.
- **Active Relaxation:** Engaging in activities that contribute to a deep sense of well-being, calm, and centeredness.
- **Rest/Recovery:** Giving your body the time it needs to recharge, rest, and recover.
- **Confidence/Personal Power:** Mental/emotional well-being and physical well-being support and sustain each other.

Next, we will jump right in with the first of the core four for the body element: nutrition and fitness...

NUTRITION AND FITNESS

The first of the core four principles of the body is "nutrition/fitness." A great way to improve our behaviors related to nutrition and fitness is by using our character strengths. Character strengths use is associated with a number of positive health behaviors, such as promoting a feeling of well-being, living an active life, pursuing enjoyable activities, healthy eating, and valuing physical fitness. While the character strength of self-regulation had the highest associations overall in a recent study, the strengths of curiosity, appreciation of beauty/excellence, gratitude, hope, humor, and zest also displayed strong connections with health behaviors.

Beyond cultivating happiness to improve your physical health, a powerful tool you have to benefit the health of your body is your fork. All calories are not equal. In his book, *The UltraMind Solution*, Dr. Mark Hyman notes that food has information that affects our genes—turning them on or off. In Dr. Hyman's words: "Food is the fastest acting and most powerful medicine you can take to change your life."[85]

Getting the amount of sleep your body needs is also paramount. Set goals for your physical fitness by regularly incorporating aerobic, strength training, and flexibility exercises. Take a brief stretch break after every 90-minute work session whenever possible—this will enable blood flow to your brain. Along with a healthy diet that is free of toxins, it's essential to hydrate—drinking about eight glasses of water on a daily basis. Being dehydrated can cause fuzzy thinking, headaches, and blood circulation problems. Performance gurus Jim Loehr and Tony Schwarz have observed, "Drinking water, we have found, is perhaps the most undervalued source of physical energy renewal."[86]

Experts agree that regular, moderate exercise is also important. Whether it's as simple as a walk in the fresh air, or a yoga class, or tennis with friends, it's important to move our bodies. According to the Harvard Medical School, "Exercising regularly, every day if possible, is the single most important thing you can do for your health. In the short term, exercise helps to control appetite, boost mood, and improve sleep. In the long term, it reduces the risk of heart disease, stroke, diabetes, dementia, depression, and many cancers. The Centers for Disease Control and Prevention (CDC) recommend the following:

For adults of all ages: At least 150 minutes of moderate aerobic exercise (like brisk walking), or 75 minutes of vigorous exercise (like running), or an equivalent mix of both every week. It's fine to break up exercise into smaller sessions as long as each one lasts at least ten minutes. Also incorporate strength-training that works all major muscle groups—legs, hips, back, abdomen, chest, shoulders, and arms—at least two days a week. Strength training may involve lifting weights, using resistance bands, or exercises like push-ups and sit-ups, in which your body weight furnishes the resistance.

For pregnant women: The guidelines for aerobic exercise are considered safe for most pregnant women. The CDC makes no recommendation for strength training. It's a good idea to review your exercise plan with your doctor.

For children: At least 60 minutes of physical activity a day, most of which should be devoted to aerobic exercise. Children should do vigorous exercise and strength training, such as push-ups or gymnastics, at least three days every week."[87]

ACTIVE RELAXATION

Let's now go to the next core principle of the body— "active relaxation." To help define active relaxation, we can consider this quote by Dr. Gretchen Kubacky: "Active relaxation is consistent with the idea of being productive, yet counter to it. What do I mean by active relaxation? I mean choosing activities that contribute to a deep sense of well-being, centeredness, calm, and good health."[88]

As we learned previously, positive psychology is the scientific study of human flourishing. You will recall that a component of this scientific field is called "embodied positive psychology."

Megan McDonough, CEO of the Wholebeing Institute, once shared with me: "The brain, body, and breath are inextricably linked. We are physiologically constructed in a way that a change in one affects a change in another. So, when you slow and deepen your breathing, especially elongating the exhale, the body relaxes. When your body relaxes, your brain releases different chemicals. Your nervous system moves from the fight or flight response to rest and digest. We are not prisoners of habits of body, breath, or brain. We can break the cycle in any of the three points."[89]

Although the benefits have been reported for many years, science continues to assert how practices that quiet the mind and calm the body benefit us profoundly. Centering practices such as reconnecting with our higher self, mindfulness, deep breathing, immersion in nature, yoga, mantras, loving kindness meditation, prayer, or other contemplative practices affect not only our psychology, but also our physiology.[90] Simply observing our breath can be a celebration of our very life, quickly and joyfully reconnecting us with our body. These restorative practices affect the body's immune system, biochemistry, metabolism, heart rate, blood pressure, and brain chemistry.[91][92]

REST AND RECOVERY

The next principle is "rest/recovery." When we think of well-being for our bodies, we tend to think more about nutrition and fitness than we do about rest and recovery. Yet, rest and recovery—giving your body time to recharge—is just as essential.

Arianna Huffington has been on a compassionate crusade to help people see the wisdom in recharging, especially as it relates to rest and recovery. With sincere concern for the welfare of others, she shares her own story of working massive hours building the *Huffington Post* website in her book *Sleep Revolution*. While juggling the phone and emails at the same time, she passed out from exhaustion, waking up in a pool of blood with a broken cheekbone and a lacerated eye. Huffington points to the irony: "We sacrifice sleep in the name of productivity, but ironically our loss of sleep, despite the extra hours we spend at work, adds up to 11 days of lost productivity per year per worker."

Below is a brief summary of science-based sleep tips shared by Huffington in her book (I highly recommend reading the entire book):

- Keep your bedroom dark, quiet, and cool (between 60 and 67 degrees).
- No electronic devices starting 30 minutes before bedtime.
- Don't charge phone next to your bed. Even better: gently escort all devices out of your bedroom.
- No caffeine after 2 p.m.
- Remember, your bed is for sleep and sex only—no work!

- Sorry, Mr. Snuffles: No pets on the bed.
- Take a hot bath with Epsom salts before bed to help calm your mind and body.
- Pajamas, nightdresses, and even special T-shirts send a sleep-friendly message to your body. If you wore it to the gym, don't wear it to bed.
- Do light stretching, deep breathing, yoga, or meditation to help your body and mind transition to sleep.
- When reading in bed, make it a real book or an e-reader that does not emit blue light. And make sure it's not work-related: novels, poetry, philosophy, anything but work.
- Ease yourself into sleep mode by drinking some chamomile or lavender tea.
- Before bed, write a list of what you are grateful for. It's a great way to make sure your blessings get the closing scene of the night.[93]

CONFIDENCE AND PERSONAL POWER

The final core principle for the body element is "confidence/personal power." The positive correlation between exercise and physical health is well documented. Yet, science is now showing an equally strong correlation between an active lifestyle, exercising regularly, and mental and emotional well-being. Interestingly, people experience an increase in confidence, among many benefits. Regular positive health habits are linked to:

- Decreased depressive symptoms
- Reduced stress/anxiety
- Improved mood
- Increased confidence[94]

Positive health habits, particularly exercise, produce endorphins, which can induce positive feelings, and increase the release of mood-elevating chemicals such as serotonin, norepinephrine, and dopamine. The positive feelings and mood that come from these healthy habits can impact the way we feel about ourselves, thus potentially increasing our self-confidence and sense of personal power.

Regular positive health habits can actually improve the way we see our body—our body image. This can spark the principle of positive progression— positive health habits increase our confidence and personal power, which in turn increase our desire to engage in positive health habits.

Below is a summary of a recent Harvard Health Publishing article that offers five strategies that can help you gain greater confidence:

- **Look Good:** Take pride in your appearance, e.g., practice good hygiene, get dressed for the day... "When you put in the effort to improve your appearance, you find that your opinion of yourself becomes more positive."
- **Learn Something:** Activities like learning to paint or play an instrument, studying a foreign language, taking dance lessons, or attending writing classes foster the desire to utilize a new skill.
- **Challenge Yourself Physically:** Find a physical challenge that you can realistically complete. For example, train for a 5K, or even walk a mile a day for a month.
- **Stay Connected:** Studies show that personal connections help reduce the risks for depression and anxiety often associated with feelings of low self-esteem—volunteering is a great way to do this.
- **Seek Help:** Group therapy or one-on-one counseling can help you work through obstacles that affect confidence. Getting help does NOT make you weak: "Never be afraid to seek professional help when you need it."[95]

We are now going to do an exercise to increase our confidence and personal power. This exercise leverages the innate wisdom of the body.

EXERCISE: PERSONAL POWER

We experience so many stressors in today's world and those stressors can influence our well-being choices—such as being in a rush and grabbing unhealthy snacks on the go, to crashing at the end of the day on the couch and mindlessly watching TV. Take a few moments to tune into your body and break out of any unhealthy cycles you may find yourself in. In your *Well-Being Workbook*, write a letter from your body to you, as if your body were talking to you. Your body has intrinsic wisdom to keep itself healthy, so ask your body what you could do to honor it:

- What does your body need from you to keep itself healthy?
- How can you best respect/honor your body?
- Why will consistently appreciating your body bring you greater joy in all aspects of your life?

You will be amazed at how quickly you intuitively know what your body needs to be at its best, because you live within your body.

RECHARGE YOUR BODY WITH STRENGTHS

Many of the 24 character strengths have been shown to improve health and well-being.[96] Here are just three examples to get you started thinking about how you can use your character strengths to recharge the body element.

PERSEVERANCE	FAIRNESS	SELF-REGULATION
Choose a new, attainable physical activity. Commit to doing it each day for one month.	Be fair to yourself by allocating time to improve your own well-being.	Create one new strengths-based behavior for improving your health and implement consistently.

EXERCISE: SETTING A STRONG GOAL

Now that we've looked at some examples of how we can use character strengths to recharge the body, let's focus on setting a sustainable goal to do just that. Here is a powerful model for a strengths-based goal process that you can use to recharge the body. It's the acronym "STRONG" with each letter representing a critical step in reaching any goal:

STRONG GOALS TOOL

S=Strengths. Power your goal by identifying which of your strengths would best be applied to the goal—this will energize the goal and you! Clearly describe the outcome you are seeking and write it down or have pictures represent it, making the description as vivid as you can. Documenting the goal is a powerful statement and commitment to yourself and others.

T=Timed. Ensure that your goal has clearly defined timeframes or milestones that allow you to check progress along the way. Don't overload—choose one or two realistic goals at a time to focus on. Build confidence through consistent gains. Plan realistic celebrations for each milestone.

R=Relevant. Does your goal have meaning and purpose and align with your ideal, long-term vision?

O=Options. Weigh all your options. Explore the potential rewards and costs of each of your goal options so that you can choose the highest leverage goal.

N=Network. Identify a support network. Have you identified all available resources (people, educational, financial, etc.)? Honestly assess the ability of family members, peers, and friends to provide support.

G=Growth. Does the goal stretch and inspire you? Grow with the goal—reflect on progress, reveal insights, and based on your insights, recalibrate when necessary. Have there been unforeseen changes in your circumstances that require a modification to the goal or that make the goal irrelevant? Be honest with yourself, make needed changes, and be open to growth.

STRONG Goals, ©2014-2021, Authentic Strengths Advantage, LLC. All rights reserved.

Take the next 15 minutes to choose a goal for recharging your body and write your goal in your *Well-Being Workbook*. Address your goal with each of the STRONG Goals steps listed above. If you are having difficulty setting a goal, you can look at your less-used strengths and consider choosing one of these strengths that you want to build—one that you believe will positively impact how you care for your body.

BODY: MINDFULNESS PRACTICE

Let's end our discussion on the element of the body with another mindfulness practice. Again, find a comfortable place where you will not be disturbed to experience and reflect on the written version of this practice below, or you can listen to the mindfulness practices at <u>AuthenticStrengths.com</u>:

Move your awareness to the area of your solar plexus or abdomen.
Imagine this corresponds with your physical health,
your personal power and confidence.
Visualize your body as strong, healthy, fit, nurtured by nutritious food,
rested, relaxed, filled with vitality.
Recharge by saying: I am empowered, healthy, strong and confident.
Take a moment and soak in the positive emotions this provides for you.

HEART

CHAPTER FOUR

HEART

"Wherever you go, go with all your heart." [97]

—CONFUCIUS

YOUR RELATIONSHIP WITH SELF AND OTHERS

Let's move on to our next element: the heart. We use the heart as a metaphor for our relationships with self and with others. Developing positive relationships and emotional intelligence can help us cultivate greater self-awareness and social-awareness.[98]

In addition, the heart is often referred to as a source of connection, or interdependence, with others. In sharp contrast, fierce independence is often praised in modern society. Look around you—in the news, in magazines, in politics, in communities, on social media—and you will see movements to separate oneself, or one's group, from others. But this disconnection can come at a high cost, as is evidenced by growing tension and the resulting stress, anxiety, and depression. Although it's healthy and necessary to care for and honor oneself, the advice to always first "look out for number one," continually putting oneself before others, can take its toll on relationships and communities, as well as dimming our own spirits through this myopic view.

Dr. Barbara Fredrickson in her book, *Love 2.0: How Our Supreme Emotion Affects Everything We Feel, Think, Do, and Become*, explains the price we sometimes pay when we lose this "heart" connection with others: "...one unfortunate side effect of rugged individualism can be a thick cocoon of self-absorption that all but blinds you to the concerns, gifts, and welfare of others."[99]

Once during a relationships class, a woman pulled me aside. She said the biggest insight for her was taking responsibility for, and better managing, her emotions. She had learned emotional intelligence skills to better present herself with a sense of clarity and self-control to others.

She had learned to use "I" statements, such as "I feel frustrated when I spend hours working alone on a task that I understood to be a team effort," rather than "you" statements, such as "You always dump the work on my shoulders, and I get no help!" Using "I" statements demonstrates taking responsibility for one's feelings while deploying the "You" statement places blame, eliciting defensiveness in the relationship.

So, in this element of the "heart," you will learn helpful relationship skills. Do you have unrealistic expectations of another person? Do you find yourself rehashing negative experiences in a way that damages your well-being? We will learn how to shift our focus to the present, where the solutions generally are found. It's ok to briefly visit the past for context, but it's not healthy to live there.

And don't underestimate the power of forgiving yourself and others, or of setting healthy boundaries. This can free you from emotional cords that may have held you hostage for years.

The following is one individual's story of healing and well-being:

This past year, I have been able to heal from many things that were holding me hostage. I wasn't able to have relationships go past a certain point. I sabotaged most of my relationships and avoided serious conversations. I discovered trauma from my past that was holding me back from being truly vulnerable and allowing my relationships to grow past a certain point. After processing these things with a professional and creating healthy boundaries, slowly I am able to let those relationships in my life grow and not ambush my connections. There is something freeing about being able to live life with a survivor mindset instead of a victim mindset.

THE HIGHER GROUND OF UNITY

Investing in our relationships promotes our own well-being in this "heart" element—lifting us to what I call "the higher ground of unity." Our connections with others extend beyond family, friends and colleagues, as we increasingly see that we are connected to people in our communities and around the world. As Dr. Martin Luther King wisely noted, "Whatever affects one directly, affects all indirectly. I can never be what I ought to be until you are what you ought to be. This is the interrelated structure of reality."[100]

Expressing gratitude and appreciation for the strengths in others does not diminish oneself, but rather elevates people, relationships, families, communities, and organizations to this higher ground of unity. Because they are social emotions, showing gratitude and appreciation to others enhances relationships, helping us to see how we've been supported and affirmed by the people in our lives.[101]

And when we strive to develop what is noble and best in ourselves, others will catch the vision and want to do the same. In fact, character strengths use has been shown to inspire others to rise to the example that has been set, to match the tone of the behavior. As Dr. Peterson and Dr. Seligman assert: "In many if not most cases, onlookers are elevated by their observation of virtuous action. Admiration is created more than jealousy because character strengths are the sorts of characteristics to which most can—and do—aspire. The more people surrounding us who are kind, or curious, or full of hope, the greater our own likelihood of acting in these ways."[102] All benefit when someone acts in accordance with his or her strengths and virtues.

HEART: CREATING A POSITIVE MINDSET

Let's check in with your mindset for the heart element. Place a mark where you
are currently on the arrow continuum for each statement related to this element.

INNER CRITIC	VS.	INNER COACH
Reject/Withdraw Love	←→	Give/Receive Love
Avoid Relationships	←→	Nurture Relationships
Conditional Self-Love	←→	Unconditional Self-Love
Unforgiving	←→	Forgiving
Overly Permissive	←→	Healthy Boundaries
Judgmental of Self/Others	←→	Compassion to Self/Others

Inner Coach vs. Inner Critic Model: Heart, ©2014-2021,
Authentic Strengths Advantage, LLC. All rights reserved.

Your inner coach offers encouragement—which comes from the Latin
word "cor" meaning "heart,"[103] or "to hearten and inspire."[104] Think about that
for a moment. It's a fundamental shift to recognize that perhaps the most important job you can take on is encouraging yourself and those around you.

In essence, your inner coach is the wisdom of your heart—the encouraging
self-talk that you can tune into. The world's revered teachings use the heart as a
metaphor for the seat of compassion, connection, human spirit, and empathy—a
place of inner knowing that can guide us through life's challenges. Your heart,
when coherent and tranquil, is like your inner coach—profoundly intelligent,
seeing more clearly than the inner critic that can plague your mind with endless
discordant and non-productive thoughts.

The key to evoking your inner coach and silencing your inner critic is to
first take the time to quiet the mind. As you fully embrace the present moment as
the "observer" of your inner world, you can connect to the wisdom that resides in
your heart. It's from this place that one hears what many refer to as the profound
"whisperings of the heart."

As stated before, centering practices such as mindfulness, yoga, deep breathing, mantras/affirmations, loving kindness meditation, prayer, or other contemplative practices affect not only our psychology, but also our physiology—including the heart—often creating a more coherent heart rhythm and more positive emotions, among other benefits. [105]

HEART: THE CORE FOUR

The core four principles of the heart element are:

- **Self-Compassion/Self-Love:** This includes self-care and self-acceptance.
- **Healthy Relationships:** This is about fulfilling connections and relationships with self and others.
- **Forgiveness:** We will explore the ability to let go of all that does not serve us.
- **Bravery/Boundaries:** We will identify appropriate boundaries that not only keep us safe, but can also help our relationships thrive.

Let's begin with the first of the core four of the heart element: self-compassion and self-love...

SELF-COMPASSION AND SELF-LOVE

The first core principle of the heart is "self-compassion/self-love." When we deal honestly with our negative emotions, we can extend genuine compassion to ourselves. This enables us to feel cared for, accepted, and secure. We are then able to shift our focus to our strengths and employ them in finding solutions. The self-produced feelings of well-being and safety deactivate the body's threat system, calming down the amygdala and mitigating the release of stress chemicals—increasing the production of positive chemicals as a counterbalance.

Positive psychologists Kristin Neff's and Christopher Germer's research on self-compassion is showing that a healthy way to manage unavoidable negative emotions is to acknowledge them while practicing self-soothing techniques. This can soften negative emotions, eventually losing their debilitating grip. Neff identifies three components of self-compassion:

- **Self-Kindness:** Being kind and understanding toward ourselves when we suffer, fail, or feel inadequate, rather than ignoring our pain or flagellating ourselves with self-criticism.

- **Common Humanity:** Recognizing we are all human, none of us is perfect, and everyone experiences loss or failure at some time in his or her life. Our frustration with not having things exactly as we want is often accompanied by an irrational sense of isolation—as if we are the only person suffering or making mistakes. This is simply not so and reminding oneself of this can be a source of comfort.

- **Mindfulness:** Taking a balanced, mindful approach to our negative emotions so that our feelings are neither suppressed nor exaggerated.[106]

HEALTHY RELATIONSHIPS

Now that we've explored self-compassion and self-love, which focuses on our relationship with self, let's shift our focus to our relationships with others. So, to delve further into how to create healthy relationships, let's define and talk about emotional intelligence.

Emotional intelligence (EQ) became popular in 1995 with psychologist Dr. Daniel Goleman's bestselling book, *Emotional Intelligence.* An extremely simplified definition of emotional intelligence could be stated as: "the capacity for recognizing our own feelings and those of others, and the ability to manage those feelings to motivate ourselves and others."[107] Dr. Goleman, the world's leading authority on emotional intelligence, proposed that being "book smart," having high IQ scores, or even graduating from Ivy League schools does not guarantee success. As a matter of fact, the highest predictor of success, Goleman found, was emotional intelligence. And guess what? Many character strengths make up emotional intelligence, such as self-regulation, social intelligence, and teamwork, just to mention a few.

What is so compelling about emotional intelligence? During a weeklong course I attended facilitated by Dr. Goleman and his wife, Tara, the importance of emotional intelligence and character strengths were reinforced. Dr. Goleman conveyed to me that the science of character strengths is so exciting to him because it brings to the surface the cherished strengths in people, helping them understand when and where they can best apply their character strengths to create their best future.[108]

Psychology Today affirms our ability to increase our EQ, making the connection between emotional intelligence and the health of our relationships:

> An emotionally intelligent individual is both highly conscious of his or her own emotional states, even negativity—frustration, sadness, or something more subtle—and able to identify and manage them. These people are also especially tuned into the emotions others experience. It's easy to see how a sensitivity to emotional signals from within and from the social environment could make one a better friend, parent, leader, or romantic partner. Fortunately, these skills can be honed.[109]

It's not about learning a script. It's about developing a new perception of reality centered on genuinely being one's best self, being a contribution to others. The key, as we learned earlier, is to approach defining moments in our relationships as a coach rather than as a critic.

Another key component to having healthy, meaningful relationships is to embrace vulnerability. In her book, *Daring Greatly: How the Courage to be Vulnerable Transforms the Way We Live, Love, Parent and Lead*, Brené Brown offers a truth about vulnerability that I believe is foundational to emotional intelligence, "Vulnerability sounds like truth and feels like courage. Truth and courage aren't always comfortable, but they're never weakness."[110] In other words, self-awareness and social awareness require the courage to be vulnerable—to relate authentically with others. Our close relationships deepen when we allow ourselves to be vulnerable. Emotional intelligence is a reflection of this kind of honest vulnerability. By being vulnerable we lower our shields and open our hearts to others, engendering mutual, genuine understanding. This involves learning to see and appreciate the authenticity in others, as well as taking the risk to be seen for one's authenticity as well.

One of the most important aspects of healthy relationships is developing empathy and compassion for others. Harvard's Making Caring Common project posts this definition of empathy on their landing page: "Empathy is at the heart of what it means to be human. It's a foundation for acting ethically, for good relationships of many kinds, for loving well, and for professional success. And its key to preventing bullying and many other forms of cruelty.

Empathy begins with the capacity to take another perspective, to walk in another's shoes. But it's not just that capacity. Salespeople, politicians, actors and marketers are often very skilled at taking other perspectives, but they may not care about others. Con [artists] and torturers take other perspectives so they can exploit people's weaknesses. Empathy includes valuing other perspectives and people. It's about perspective-taking and compassion."[111]

In conclusion, we can draw inspiration from the four main points of a Harvard Medical School article titled, "Can Relationships Boost Longevity and Well-Being?" They are as follows:

1. Social connections are good for health
2. Loneliness can be toxic
3. Relationship quality matters
4. Good relationships can protect our brains[112]

FORGIVENESS

The third core principle of the heart is "forgiveness." Research suggests that forgiveness can improve our well-being, reduce our stress levels, lower our blood pressure, lessen gastrointestinal and other bodily pains, boost our immune system—benefitting our well-being.[113] In addition, forgiveness has been linked to increased positive emotions, especially when we forgive someone close to us.[114] Juxtapose this to holding a grudge, which has the opposite effect overall.[115]

Forgiveness also builds relationships because when we let go of hurt or disappointment, we are more likely to cooperate with others. Forgiveness increases trust in our relationships, bringing us closer together and stopping the toxic downward spiral that can lead us to walk away from important relationships. Most importantly, forgiveness elevates everyone to experience life on a higher plane. We are inspired to be more forgiving when others extend forgiveness to us.

Dr. Fred Luskin, one of the world's leading researchers on forgiveness and Director of the Stanford University Forgiveness Projects, uses forgiveness therapy with people around the world, including those who suffered the attacks on the World Trade Center on 9/11. His work and his book *Forgive for Good*, have helped people in their personal lives, and also in corporate, medical, legal and religious settings. Dr. Luskin has beautifully summed up the myriad benefits of forgiveness as follows: "The practice of forgiveness has been shown to reduce anger, hurt, depression and stress, and leads to greater feelings of hope, peace, compassion and self-confidence. Practicing forgiveness leads to healthy relationships as well as physical health. It also influences our attitude which opens the heart to kindness, beauty, and love."[116]

Below is a summary of the nine steps to forgiveness that Dr. Luskin offers on his website:

1. Know exactly how you feel about what happened and be able to articulate what about the situation is not OK. Then, tell a trusted couple of people about your experience.

2. Make a commitment to yourself to do what you have to do to feel better. Forgiveness is for you and not for anyone else.

3. Forgiveness does not necessarily mean reconciliation with the person that hurt you, nor condoning of their action. What you are after is to find peace. Forgiveness can be defined as the "peace and understanding that come from blaming that which has hurt you less, taking the life experience less personally, and changing your grievance story."

4. Get the right perspective on what is happening. Recognize that your primary distress is coming from the hurt feelings, thoughts, and physical upset you are suffering now, not what offended you or hurt you two minutes —or ten years—ago. Forgiveness helps to heal those hurt feelings.

5. At the moment you feel upset, practice a simple stress management technique to soothe your body's flight-or-fight response.

6. Give up expecting things from other people, or your life, that they do not choose to give you. Recognize the "unenforceable rules" you have for your health or how you or other people must behave. Remind yourself that you can hope for health, love, peace, and prosperity and work hard to get them.

7. Put your energy into looking for another way to get your positive goals met than through the experience that has hurt you. Instead of mentally replaying your hurt, seek out new ways to get what you want.

8. Remember that a life well lived is your best revenge. Instead of focusing

on your wounded feelings, and thereby giving the person who caused you pain power over you, learn to look for the love, beauty, and kindness around you. Forgiveness is about personal power.

9. Re-write your grievance story to remind you of the heroic choice to forgive.[117]

After studying the latest research on forgiveness, I've synthesized the best thinking I could find, while combining it with character strengths, into the following easy to remember, visual tool below. I call it the Authentic Forgiveness Tool, and it's my sincere hope that more of us will take the time to give ourselves the gift of forgiving—ourselves and others. Take a moment to review this tool and envision using it in specific situations in your life. Consider any resentments that you may have been holding onto that, if let go, would enable you to reclaim your inner peace.

AUTHENTIC FORGIVENESS TOOL

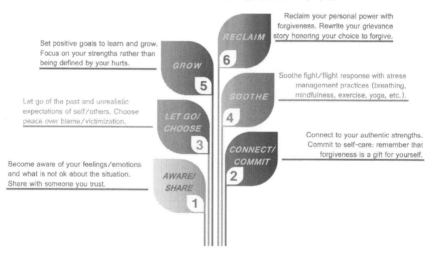

Inspired by: Luskin, Dr. Fred, The Stanford Forgiveness Project: Effects of Group Forgiveness Intervention on Perceived Stress, State and Trait, Anger, Symptoms of Stress, Self-Reported Health and Forgiveness, Forgive for Good, 9 Steps (2006); Saffarinia, Majid and Mohammadi, Narges and Afshar, Hamid (2016) The role of interpersonal forgiveness in resilience and severity of pain in chronic pain patients. Journal of Fundamentals of Mental Health; REACH Forgiveness of Others by Everett Worthington.

EXERCISES: FORGIVENESS & LETTING GO

Is there someone or some situation that you could benefit from forgiving? Take the time to write a forgiveness note, although you don't need to send it. That's entirely up to you. Sometimes just writing it out on paper can help you release resentment. Feel the positive emotions of letting go flow through you—are you experiencing freedom, peace, contentment, ease, equanimity, love? Savor these new positive emotions as they "undo" any past negativity you have been holding onto. Write down your insights in your *Well-Being Workbook*.

Another "letting go" exercise that has worked for many people is taking time to visualize the other person's higher self and imagine that you are talking to them. Using "I" statements, explain to the other person's higher self how you feel. It's helpful to purge the old feelings, and in the process, it can help you to better understand your emotions and reactions. It's also a helpful way of honoring yourself and relieving pent up anger and frustration.

BRAVERY AND BOUNDARIES

The final core principle of the heart element is a natural follow-up to forgiveness—"bravery/boundaries." As we practice forgiveness of ourselves and others, letting go of past grievances that no longer serve us, our boundaries often come into focus. We find ourselves examining what works for us and what doesn't, and setting healthy boundaries often requires exercising our bravery. Remember that the Latin word for the heart is "cor" which is also closely related to the word: "courage." This is where the word "encouragement" comes from—so we can see the connection to bravery and healthy boundaries, and how these help us live a vibrant, whole life—positively impacting our well-being.[118]

Millions of people resonate with Dr. Brené Brown because of her common-sense wisdom. She provides this straightforward definition of boundaries: "simply our lists of what's okay and what's not okay." Brown asserts that it makes sense for all ages in all situations to set healthy boundaries, and she expands on the connection between bravery and boundaries—in Brown's words: "When we combine the courage to make clear what works for us and what doesn't with the compassion to assume people are doing their best, our lives change. Yes, there will be people who violate our boundaries, and this will require that we continue to hold those people accountable. But when we're living in our integrity, we're strengthened by the self-respect that comes from the honoring of our boundaries, rather than being flattened by disappointment and resentment."[119]

Many people who have divorced later resolve to set better boundaries in their next marriage, such as the following colleague mentioned to me:

> I wish I had practiced better boundaries in my first marriage. It would have helped me to either leave sooner, or to recognize what was unacceptable behavior. Now, in my work as a marriage and family therapist, I often see people blindsided by their spouse leaving them. The person leaving is literally "snapping" after years of not speaking up. I believe that healthy boundary setting is preventative, because it helps relationships, can save marriages, and reduces resentment. It may be hard to voice our boundaries and help those around us know what our healthy boundaries look like, but it's actually kinder to others to be clear. If others don't know how we feel, there can be a lot of assuming and misunderstanding. Many people think setting boundaries is rude, but I have learned that one can state firm boundaries with a kind voice and a genuine intent to build and heal the relationship.

I've discussed this topic of boundaries with several of my colleagues and reviewed considerable research on creating healthy boundaries. The result of this exploration is the following tool I've developed to help people remember the key elements of healthy boundaries.

AUTHENTIC BOUNDARIES TOOL

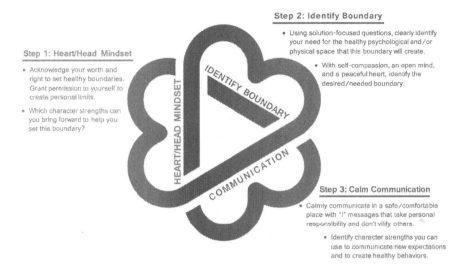

Step 2: Identify Boundary

- Using solution-focused questions, clearly identify your need for the healthy psychological and/or physical space that this boundary will create.

- With self-compassion, an open mind, and a peaceful heart, identify the desired/needed boundary.

Step 1: Heart/Head Mindset

- Acknowledge your worth and right to set healthy boundaries. Grant permission to yourself to create personal limits.

- Which character strengths can you bring forward to help you set this boundary?

Step 3: Calm Communication

- Calmly communicate in a safe/comfortable place with "I" messages that take personal responsibility and don't vilify others.

- Identify character strengths you can use to communicate new expectations and to create healthy behaviors.

Inspired by: Dr. Henry Cloud and Dr. John Townsend, Boundaries (2017); Buck, Chad, Establishing Effective Personal Boundaries, Vanderbilt University Faculty and Staff Health and Wellness (2015, 2016); Pury, Cynthia, and Shane Lopez. The Psychology of Courage: Modern Research on an Ancient Virtue. The Psychology of Courage: Modern Research on an Ancient Virtue. Washington, DC, U.S.: American Psychological Association, (2010); Dr. Brené Brown "3 Ways to Set Boundaries." Oprah. com; and Lindsay Holmes "10 Great Things that Happen When You Set Boundaries." Huffington Post. April 4, 2016.

EXERCISE: BOUNDARIES

Spend some time identifying and writing down your own healthy boundaries in your *Well-Being Workbook*. You may want to call forth some of your strengths, such as social intelligence, kindness, teamwork, perspective, fairness, etc. as you plan in advance how you will handle challenging interactions with grace. As Brené Brown has said in her blog, "Clear is kind, unclear is unkind."[120]

You can begin by answering the following questions:

- Balancing your bravery with compassion for others, how can you best express your healthy boundaries to the people in your life when the situation requires it?
- Which of your character strengths will you call forward to help you do

this, and how do you plan to use those character strengths in a way that is kind yet firm?

RECHARGE YOUR HEART WITH STRENGTHS

Let's now consider a few ideas on how you can recharge the heart element. Here are just some examples utilizing your character strengths, such as your strengths of social intelligence, love, and forgiveness.

SOCIAL INTELLIGENCE
Consider your impact on others before speaking/acting.

LOVE
Give a sincere compliment to a different person (including yourself) each day for a week.

FORGIVENESS
Forgive past offenses so that your heart can be free of resentment.

CONNECT, CARE, CREATE

As we've learned so far, everyone experiences challenges and disappointments; therefore, negative emotions are an unavoidable part of life. Negative emotions are often experienced like a wave. They can be powerful as they build and crest, but they typically don't stay at their height; they eventually flow back to normal. If they are stuffed (like damming a river), they can become stagnant and toxic, and the emotion levels, like water levels behind a dam, can remain high.

I've synthesized what I found to be the best techniques to manage negative emotions into what I call the "Connect-Care-Create Tool." This tool can help you process common negative emotions associated with personal and professional disappointments, losses, or failures.

- First, because your brain tends to exaggerate a single event and get stuck in an endless cycle of rumination, this process begins with focusing on your body, which helps stop the cycle by giving your brain something new to focus on.
- Second, it prompts you toward self-care and self-compassion by helping you accept that negative emotions are a part of life.
- Third, this process helps you learn how to transform a negative emotion by using your strengths as a lens to address the issue, thus creating a new

positive emotion(s) to undo the effect of the negative emotion.

In practicing this tool, people report a sense of relief, liberation, and a freedom from rumination that opens them to real growth. The most encouraging part of this approach is that you can learn to productively process negative emotions. After all, you are the one person in your life that is always around when you are feeling negative emotions, so why not learn to deliver the best antidote?

Disclaimer: *Some negative emotions, like those rooted in mental health issues, substance abuse, abusive environments, etc., may require the help of a medical professional or therapist. Please seek appropriate help.*

Let's take the next five minutes to experience this tool:

CONNECT, CARE, CREATE TOOL

- **Connect** - Get in a comfortable seated position. Become mindful of and connect to a negative emotion you are feeling or have felt in the past. Notice all aspects of the emotion without judging it, shaming it, or avoiding it. Just let yourself observe it truthfully and objectively, while practicing self-compassion. Where in your body do you feel the emotion most?
- **Care** - Practice self-care. Relax the area where you are holding the negative emotion (your stomach, shoulders, heart, back, lungs, etc.), and imagine it dissolving like an ice cube in warm water. Send yourself compassion, reminding yourself that everyone experiences difficult moments, loss, mistakes, and failure. Reassure yourself that all will be well, that you will give yourself the support you need to get through this experience, and that you will take the steps to better the situation.
- **Create** - Identify a character strength(s) to help you transform this negative emotion and create a positive shift in perspective. How can you learn and grow from this experience? What new positive emotions are you feeling now...hope, forgiveness, love, perspective, kindness, self-regulation? Notice your negative emotion gradually dissipate and lose its power over you as new positive emotions are created in its place.

Connect, Care, Create Tool, ©2014-2021, Authentic Strengths Advantage, LLC.
All rights reserved.

How did that experience go for you? What did you learn? Take the next few minutes to capture your insights in your *Well-Being Workbook*.

HEART: MINDFULNESS PRACTICE

Let's end our discussion on the heart element with a mindfulness practice. Again, you can choose to read, experience, and reflect on the written words below, or you can listen to the mindfulness practices at AuthenticStrengths.com:

Move your attention to the cherished area of your heart.
This corresponds with self-compassion and self-love, with your relationships,
your ability to forgive and to exercise courage.
Place your hand over your heart, honoring,
loving, and sending compassion to yourself,
while appreciating others.
Breathing in, invite healthy, harmonious, trusting, relationships into your life.
Choose joy in the journey.
Breathing out fully, forgive yourself and others—
letting go of all that does not serve you,
identifying appropriate boundaries.
Recharge as you say: I am in healthy relationships
with myself and with others, and I find joy in life.
Take a moment to enjoy the positive emotions this generates within you.

CONTRIBUTION

CHAPTER FIVE

CONTRIBUTION

"I alone cannot change the world,
but I can cast a stone across the waters to create many ripples."[121]

—MOTHER TERESA

YOUR UNIQUE CONTRIBUTIONS

Our next element is contribution. One reason many New Year resolutions fail is because they are focused only on "self" and leave out the important element of contributing to others. Without the tie to others, they don't have enough long-term motivation to keep us going. We are social by nature—we thrive when those around us thrive. If I see myself as being a "contribution" to others rather than just accomplishing a goal for myself, then whatever I do, it's powered by something bigger than myself. Creating value and fulfillment for the recipient of my contribution in turn creates value and fulfillment for me, launching a positive upward spiral.[122] It's the law of reciprocity—what goes around comes around. Below are some benefits of contribution:

- Energizes your goals as you use your strengths
- Creates value and fulfillment for the recipient(s) of your actions and for you
- Serves as an antidote to unproductive competition and comparison
- Fills your efforts with meaning and genuine value

For example, if your goal is to improve your health, ask yourself: "Why do I want to do this?" Which is more compelling: losing weight to look better, or becoming healthy so that you have more energy to participate in activities with those you love? Learning to love, value, and take care of yourself is a powerful growth experience and motivator. As you begin to truly value yourself, you will also begin to see how you can be a contribution to others, which then makes getting and staying healthy deeply compelling.

When we work from the desire to make things better not only for ourselves, but also for others, obstacles seem to vanish, and unpleasant tasks become more pleasant. Those negative, critical, judging internal voices and the rants of our inner critic fall away. We notice what we can give, and that focus becomes a freeing and joyful experience.

I remember the first time I shared these concepts on television. As I drove to the TV station, my clammy hands gripped the steering wheel, and I could feel my heart pounding in my chest as I mentally reviewed what I would say. I took a couple of deep breaths, and I said out loud, "Fatima, just 'be' a contribution today. Think only about helping people today and everything will fall into place."

That small adjustment transported me from fear of failure to simply wanting to get helpful information across to people. Like everyone, I get caught up in everyday pressures to perform, but when I'm immersed in using my strengths to contribute, the performance anxiety melts away and I get the deep satisfaction that comes from giving to others—the world becomes a much less complicated place.

When we ask, "What are the needs I see around me?" what begins to emerge is the contribution we can make, the service we can render. When this service is grounded in and powered by the most authentic part of ourselves, our character strengths, we are in the position to make a valuable contribution. The best solutions or contributions in society, in business, and in personal life have emerged when people apply their strengths to serving a need. And it's an added bonus that some sources show people who give service or contribute to others in a meaningful way may live on average ten years longer![123] It seems easy on the surface, but oftentimes we get so busy in day-to-day life that we don't even know what we are passionate about anymore. We have disconnected from those strengths that enliven us.

A friend shared this example: "One way my family has served is by taking meals to others needing a boost of some kind. I learned this during my own childhood. It came natural to my parents and grandparents to serve those around them no matter who they were. My grandma would spend hours creating mouthwatering dishes for us and others. My dad can remember a time or two when my grandma would prepare a really nice meal for a neighbor and their family might eat something not quite as grand but still delicious. I've witnessed the joy that filled my elders each time they served others. Now I'm able to teach my kids to serve. It's fun watching them experience the happiness and peace of mind that comes into their lives as they help others."

Service renews us on a deep level, and the personal benefits we reap are an added bonus. It literally improves our health. Research shows that those who are connected to their communities and give back experience a boost in their immune systems, their wounds heal faster, and they catch colds and other infections less frequently.[124]

How do we bring our passion to contribute back into our day-to-day lives? Ask yourself what is happening around you that you care about deeply—in your relationships, family, community, workplace? Answering such questions is a step toward reconnecting with your authentic strengths and enhancing your well-being.

CONTRIBUTION: CREATING A POSITIVE MINDSET

Let's check in with our contribution mindset. With this mindset, we work from the desire to make things better for others, which helps obstacles vanish and unpleasant tasks become more pleasant. The inner critic's tirades begin to fall away. Place a mark where you are currently on the arrow continuum for each statement about the contribution mindset.

INNER CRITIC	VS.	INNER COACH
Work = Draining	←——→	Work = Energizing
Disconnected	←——→	Connected
Disengaged	←——→	Engaged
Lacks Purpose	←——→	Purposeful
Stagnant/Stifled	←——→	Achievement
Self-Absorbed	←——→	Contribution-Oriented

Inner Coach vs. Inner Critic Model: Contribution, ©2014-2021,
Authentic Strengths Advantage, LLC. All rights reserved.

CONTRIBUTION: THE CORE FOUR

Now let's do a quick review of the four core principles for contribution. They are:

- **Calling/Career:** Experiencing an alignment between our work and who we are at our core is fulfilling.
- **Engagement:** Using character strengths boosts engagement in meaningful tasks.
- **Accomplishment:** Gaining mastery, completing priorities, and achieving goals provides a sense of accomplishment.
- **Positive Impact:** Emanating and contributing to positivity that impacts self and others creates a positive contagion.

Let's begin with the first one from the list above, calling/career...

CALLING AND CAREER

In his book *Happiness—Unlocking the Mysteries of Psychological Wealth*, Ed Diener talks about our outlook on work (this applies whether we work outside the home or contribute to our loved ones inside the home as a caregiver or parent) and how it can affect our happiness, our effectiveness, and ultimately our well-being. Based on his extensive research, Diener describes three orientations to work: we can see work as a job, a career, or a calling, which I've paraphrased below:

- **Job:** When we see work as a job, we view leisure as more important, we are primarily motivated by money, we would not recommend the work unless required, we do what we are told, and we look forward to the end of each task or shift.
- **Career:** When we see work as a career, we might enjoy the work, we are motivated by recognition, we may recommend the work, we think a lot about vacations, we take initiative to impress supervisors, and we work hard for possible advancement.
- **Calling:** In contrast, when we see work as a calling, we want to make meaningful contributions, we recommend the work, we think about work even off the clock, we work hard because we find the work rewarding, and doing it well is intrinsically motivating.[125]

So, why don't we raise the quality of our lives by finding ways to utilize our strengths more in our contributions to others, transforming whatever work we are doing (whether inside or outside our home) into a calling? This is when our work truly becomes a contribution, and we take joy in our work. By doing this, we are putting ourselves in a state conducive to flow—the positive, focused activities that feed creativity and increase our capacities. People who see their work as a calling are most likely to feel a deep alignment between their work and who they are as a person. They feel their work is integral to their life and identity. These people have an emotional connection, a sense of purpose, and a desire to make a meaningful contribution through their work.[126]

ENGAGEMENT

Have you ever built a rock sculpture, or stacked stones (also known as a "cairn")? Did you notice your complete absorption and focus on what you were building? Your mind probably wasn't wandering—you were likely focused on the task and not on anything else—completely involved in placing the next rock on your sculpture.

Mihaly CsikzentMihaly, the psychologist credited with having popularized the concept of flow, describes flow as: "...being completely involved in an activity for its own sake. The ego falls away. Time flies. Every action, movement, and thought follows inevitably from the previous one, like playing jazz. Your whole being is involved, and you're using your skills to the utmost."[127] Understanding how to enter and maintain the flow state is a great way to enjoy the activities we get engaged in.

In positive psychology, flow is the mental state in which a person performing a task is fully immersed in a feeling of energized focus, full involvement, and enjoyment in the process of the activity. In essence, flow is characterized by complete absorption in what one does. Achieving flow is often referred to as "being in the zone" and enables high performance.

So, to summarize, people who experience flow tend to report the following:

- **Energized Focus:** Being completely involved in the task and laser-focused.
- **Meaning/Passion:** A feeling of ecstasy, as if outside everyday reality. Feeling part of something larger than self.
- **Challenging yet Doable:** Being challenged by the task, but not anxious or worried. Knowing that the activity is doable, and that one's skills are adequate for the task.
- **Timelessness:** Being thoroughly focused on the present, as hours seem to pass by like minutes.
- **Motivated from Within:** Whatever produces flow becomes its own reward.[128]

ACCOMPLISHMENT

The third core principle of contribution is "accomplishment." Accomplishment is the "A" in "PERMA," which we learned about at the beginning of this book. As Dr. Seligman points out: "Accomplishment, also known as achievement, mastery, or competence, means that we have worked towards and reached our goals, achieved mastery over an endeavor, and had the self-motivation to complete what we set out to do."[129]

When we devote ourselves to a specific task or goal, "time" actually becomes more meaningful. A goal can be enjoyed when it's accomplished, yet it can also be savored throughout the process of attaining it. Our feelings about accomplishment can be retrospective as we look into our past and note meaningful moments throughout our past that are marked by achievements.

We can also spot our top strengths by focusing on some of our most significant accomplishments in our lives. Positive psychologist David Pollay writes: "This makes it possible for you to see a pattern in your life: you will discover that many of your greatest achievements were made possible by engaging your top strengths. Accomplishment helps you to spot the underlying patterns of your personal strengths and how they have contributed to your successes in life. This is dynamite insight about yourself and your abilities—yours to freely use for the next challenge and goal to be accomplished."[130]

A great way to motivate ourselves to achieve future goals is to visualize those goals through savoring, which we discussed during the chapter about the element of abundance. In the book *Make Your Goals Come Alive through Imagery*, author J.M. Yeager talks about savoring-in-advance by creating images of future goals with drawings, photos, articles, and quotes.[131] It also helps to imagine and savor the feelings we will experience when we accomplish our goals.

One parent shared the following example with me: "I've enjoyed watching my kids create vision boards on their walls. When my oldest was five, he wanted a specific Lego set. We printed out the picture of it and he did household jobs for me and his relatives to earn the money to buy the Lego set. It was so exciting to see him, even at such a young age, make the connection between having a clear goal, visualizing it, and mapping out what to do to achieve his goal. Now after years of doing this, he is working on earning money for a motorcycle. He has been mowing lawns for a few summers and doing chores to earn the money for his very own motorcycle."

When we take time to enjoy a new accomplishment, it can boost well-being, help us recognize our strengths, and motivate us toward creating even more of these positive experiences in the future.

POSITIVE IMPACT

The fourth and final core principle of contribution is "positive impact." Recall a time when someone had a positive impact on you. For example, perhaps you were having a bad day, so your friend who tends to be upbeat and who often encourages you, came over to lift your spirits. While you visited with this friend, you were influenced by their pervasive positive mood. Or maybe you can remember a time when you had a positive impact on others through your meaningful, helpful contributions at work, or within your family.

The converse is also true; we and others can have a negative impact on situations and people. If we are emanating fearful, angry, or malicious thoughts, emotions, and actions, then we can negatively impact not only ourselves, but those we interact with as well.

It's important to choose wisely so that our contributions will be helpful, hopeful, and meaningful, producing a positive contagion and making a positive impact around us. Ultimately, we are each responsible for our own inner world, which in turn, can influence people and situations in our outer world.

We are all connected; therefore, we can each contribute to the well-being of the whole. I was inspired by the wise and optimistic words of Rollin McCraty, PhD, HeartMath Institute's Director of Research who is heading up their Inter-connectivity Research Project, when he wrote: "I believe humanity is at a unique point in its evolutionary history of consciousness. We now have an opportunity and the intelligence to make more empowered choices to create a cooperative and harmoniously connected world."[132]

So, as you consider the positive impact you want to make in your personal and work life, also take time to reflect on your motivation, aligning it with your sense of "true north." Are your motives powered by your highest self? As Mother Teresa has reminded us, "Do things for people not because of who they are or what they'll do in return, but because of who you are."[133] You are in the driver's seat of the positive impact you choose to make wherever you go.

RECHARGE YOUR CONTRIBUTIONS WITH STRENGTHS

Here are just three of many possible ways to recharge the contribution element with your character strengths.

PERSPECTIVE	LEADERSHIP	TEAMWORK
Make a list of benefits you and others could receive from your contributions.	Research inspiring leaders who have similar top strengths as you.	Work collaboratively on a project with someone new.

EXERCISE: MOTIVATION

Let's take a few minutes to engage in a powerful exercise about motivation. You can capture your insights related to the following questions in your *Well-Being Workbook*:

- What are your deepest values?
- What motivates you?
- What is your vision, your unique contribution that you would like to make?
- How can you empower that contribution with your strengths?

Go inward as you answer these questions and reconnect with your best self. It takes courage and commitment to find your voice and to design your future. The payoff is worthwhile, however, as you emerge with an aligned sense of motivation to make your unique contributions.

CONTRIBUTION: MINDFULNESS PRACTICE

Let's end our exploration of the element of contribution with a mindfulness practice. Again, find a quiet place where you will not be disturbed to experience this mindfulness practice below—either by mindfully reading it or listening to the mindfulness practices at AuthenticStrengths.com:

Move your awareness to the area of your throat.
Imagine that this corresponds with your unique contributions to the world, your voice.
Envision yourself excelling in meaningful contributions,
fully engaged and enthusiastic to share your gifts and accomplish your goals.
Recharge by saying: I am a unique and positive contribution to the world.
Take a moment to linger in the positive emotions this calls forth within you.

MIND

CHAPTER SIX

MIND

"The sky is not the limit. Your mind is."

—AUTHOR UNKNOWN

YOUR MIND

Let's move to the next element: the mind. There are tremendous benefits to recharging the mind, all of which contribute to our overall well-being. Mind or intellectual strengths, such as creativity, curiosity, love of learning, perspective, and open-mindedness, can boost well-being because they involve the acquisition and use of information in effective ways. As Bruce H. Lipton, PhD, has said, "Your perspective is always limited by how much you know. Expand your knowledge and you will transform your mind."[134] Mind-related strengths might also help people see life in general as an interesting experience, helping them approach living in a more engaged way. In addition, they may encourage well-being by enabling us to:

- Think things through
- Examine issues from all sides
- Broaden one's perspective on any given situation
- Discern the best solutions going forward[135]

The element of the mind is also related to the work we do, how we engage in life, and our attitudes toward learning. The average person will spend 90,000 hours working in their lifetime.[136] That's a long time if you're unfulfilled or disengaged. The brain is like a muscle; if we don't use it, it will atrophy. In fact, in a famous study of the brains of retired Catholic nuns autopsied after their deaths in their 80s and 90s, several showed lesions on the brain associated with Alzheimer's disease, yet they had not exhibited symptoms of the disease. The researchers determined that their high levels of engagement with community and continuing to strive to learn new things literally saved them from the dementia associated with the disease.[137]

In the first few years of life, one million new connections are made every second. The average human brain has 86 billion neurons with as many as 1,000 trillion connections, but that number can dwindle as we age.[138] The best way to grow more connections is to take up a challenging activity that's new to you, such as learning new technology, music, or a foreign language. Flex your brain "muscle" to keep those neurons firing and to make new connections. Challenges should offer novelty and fun. Strive to learn something new.

According to one study, taking piano lessons for even four months can improve performance on math tests by an average of 27 percent.[139] Some suggestions to renew yourself mentally might be taking time to read more, enrolling in courses that interest you, or exploring hobbies that expand your mind while bringing you joy.

MIND: CREATING A POSITIVE MINDSET

Let's do a mindset check about the element of the mind. Indicate on the arrows below where you are currently and consider where you would like to be over time. As the observer of your own thoughts, you may begin to recognize debilitating negative thoughts trying to sabotage your connection to your inner coach. Counter critical thoughts by thinking of your strengths you can tap into, and by focusing on those strengths best-suited to the opportunity or challenge you face.

INNER CRITIC	VS.	INNER COACH
Closed-Minded	⟷	Open-Minded
Fixed Mindset	⟷	Growth Mindset
Afraid to Fail	⟷	Solution-Oriented
Self-Deceptive	⟷	Self-Aware
Either/Or Thinking	⟷	Unlimited Possibilities
Know-it-All	⟷	Lifelong Learner
Foolishness	⟷	Reasoning/Discernment

Inner Coach vs. Inner Critic Model: Mind, ©2014-2021,
Authentic Strengths Advantage, LLC. All rights reserved.

MIND: THE CORE FOUR

For this "mind" element, I've drawn from leading neuroscience resources, among them, Stanford University's Design Thinking model,[140] as well as from enduring traditions to better understand how to optimize one's mind. The goal is to help you with evidence-based tools that highlight the mind's potential. In this element, you will learn about the latest research in how the mind functions at its best and in harmony with all aspects of yourself—providing clarity, solutions, and enhancing your overall well-being.

The four core principles for the mind are:

- **Open-Mindedness/Reasoning:** We must first understand any need or opportunity by being open to new information—intentionally brainstorming and gathering various diverse perspectives before we can filter through, better understand, and begin organizing solutions.
- **Imagination/Ideation:** This is the stage where we explore solutions with all the information we have gathered.
- **Wisdom/Insight:** Wisdom is experiential by nature—as we test our ideas with our life experiences, we assimilate this into an evolved inner knowing called wisdom or insight.

- **Lifelong Learning/Curiosity:** This is a continuous growth approach to life that lasts a lifetime.

Let's dive right in and explore the first of the core four principles for the mind element: "open-mindedness/reasoning."

OPEN-MINDEDNESS AND REASONING

In this book, there's a reason we explored the heart element before the mind element. The Stanford University Design Thinking model points to empathy (similar to compassion discussed in the heart element) as the beginning of open-mindedness because empathy involves understanding ours and others' needs through listening and observing.[141] This opens our minds to find solutions. Therefore, I call the first core principle for the mind "open-mindedness/reasoning."

VIA also defines the strength of open-mindedness/judgment similarly.[142] According to VIA's definition: "Able to change one's mind in the light of evidence, remaining open to other arguments and perspectives...a very thinking-oriented character strength...it counteracts faulty thinking, such as favoring your current views or favoring ideas that are considered the dominant view, and therefore giving less attention to the less-dominant view. It's the willingness to search actively for evidence against your favored beliefs, plans, or goals and to weigh all of the evidence fairly when it's available."[143]

In addition, reasoning is an important skill a person uses when engaging in logical thinking. So, what is logical thinking? In the recent article, "The Best Way to Strengthen Your Logical Thinking Skills," logical thinking is defined as "the act of analyzing a situation and coming up with a sensible solution. Similar to critical thinking, logical thinking requires the use of reasoning skills to study a problem objectively, which will allow you to make a rational conclusion about how to proceed. When you use the facts available to you to address a problem you may be facing at work, for example, you are using logical reasoning skills..."[144]

Why is the skill of reasoning important to develop? Reasoning can help us think through important decisions, solve problems, ideate, and choose worthwhile goals. As your reasoning skills improve, your ability to find solutions that benefit you also increases. To build your reasoning skills, there are several methods you can consider:

- Engage in hobbies that build your creativity.
- Learn to ask good questions and why questioning is so important.
- Connect with others and learn from different life perspectives/experiences.
- Analyze the outcomes, both intended and unintended, of your potential decisions.[145]

In addition, it's helpful to note that strong critical thinkers demonstrate the following characteristics:

- Inquisitiveness with regard to a wide range of issues
- Concern to become and remain well-informed
- Attentive to opportunities to use critical thinking
- Self-confidence in one's own abilities to reason
- Open-mindedness regarding divergent worldviews
- Flexibility in considering alternatives and opinions
- Alertness to likely future events in order to anticipate their consequences
- Understanding of the opinions of other people
- Fair-mindedness when reasoning
- Honesty in facing one's own biases, prejudices, stereotypes, or egocentric tendencies
- Prudence in suspending, making, or altering judgments
- Willingness to reconsider and revise views where honest reflection suggests that change is warranted[146]

IMAGINATION AND IDEATION

The next core principle is "imagination/ideation." As human beings, one of the greatest gifts we have is to imagine outcomes, solutions, and a better future. Imagination and ideation are human capacities that are tied to our ability to continuously grow, improve, and learn. As John Maynard Keynes has said: "Ideas shape the course of history."[147]

Dr. Stephen R. Covey referred to imagination as a unique human gift each of us possesses and asserted that all human beings have the ability to access their imagination—what varies is how often one is using that gift.[148]

Ideation involves exploring potential solutions by generating a large quantity of ideas—the emphasis being on quantity rather than quality—which encourages a broadening of perspective, an ability to look beyond the obvious, and a willingness to hear and embrace a range of ideas from a diverse group of sources.

Creativity is at the heart of imagination and ideation, yet many people believe they lack this strength. American author Julia Cameron, best known for her immensely popular book *The Artist's Way*, states plainly: "There's no such thing as a non-creative person."[149] As one of the 24 character strengths, the message is the same—it's not a matter of having the character strength of creativity or not, but rather whether one is *using* the strength of creativity. This is an important and powerful paradigm shift—all of us are creative beings and creativity is a strength that can be built through consistent practice and use.

Why is creativity important to well-being? We learn from Dr. Cathi Malchiodi in her *Psychology Today* article: "Researchers considered more than 100 studies and concluded that creative expression has a powerful impact on health and well-being...Most of these studies concur that participation and/or engagement in the arts have a variety of outcomes including a decrease in depressive symptoms, an increase in positive emotions, reduction in stress responses, and, in some cases, even improvements in immune system functioning."[150]

Creativity is increasingly being validated as a potent mind-body approach to a variety of challenges throughout one's lifespan. The outcomes seem to support what humans have presumed for millennia—that creative expression is beneficial. Malchiodi points to Dr. Mihaly CsikszentMihaly's seminal Ted Talk: "When we are involved in creativity, we feel that we are living more fully than during the rest of life."[151]

Imagination, ideation, and creativity also help us to look outside of our current circumstances to envision positive solutions. For example, sometimes we think our current challenging circumstances will last forever. This can be discouraging. To counter this, we can use our imagination, ideation, and creativity to help us to look beyond the clouds and to envision where the sun will once again be peeking through. Below are some strategies:

- **Positive Emotions/Mood**: Dr. Barbara Frederickson, who studies positive emotions, suggests that positive emotions are evolutionarily adaptive because they trigger a broadening of our mental state and are shown to improve well-being.[152] Examples of how to evoke positive emotions could be to listen to your favorite music, to read something inspiring, or to appreciate something or someone dear to you before engaging in a creative or imaginative task.[153] Researchers have found that study participants in a happy mood out-performed participants in a negative or neutral mood on tasks requiring creative solutions.[154]
- **Energized Focus**: Focus and hard work are often prerequisites for creativity. An example of this is making the commitment and following through to diligently work on your creative solution to completion.
- **Time Management**: People are much less curious, imaginative, and creative when they are under time pressure. Managing time well allows space for curiosity, imagination, ideation, and creativity to thrive. An example of this might be setting aside ample time in your day for ideas to flow, rather than rushing through creative tasks.

These strategies above can open you to new solutions and enhance your well-being.

WISDOM AND INSIGHT

The next core principle of the mind is "wisdom/insight." Again, we see a synergistic alignment with the Stanford University Design Thinking model, because wisdom and insight are related to testing creative solutions, since life is experiential, and the result of our life experiences and learning is wisdom and insight.[155]

First, let's take a deeper look at wisdom. Dr. Ben Dean of the University of Pennsylvania defines wisdom as, "the ability to take stock of life in large terms, in ways that make sense to oneself and others." He explains: "Wisdom is the product of knowledge and experience, but it's more than the accumulation of information. It's the coordination of this information and its deliberate use to improve well-being...wisdom allows the individual to listen to others, to evaluate what they say, and then offer them good (sage) advice...Wisdom is a positive predictor of successful aging. In fact, wisdom is more robustly linked to the well-being of older people than objective life circumstances such as physical health, financial well-being, and physical environment."[156]

Dr. Dean wrote an article, in which he shared a list of wisdom-building activities compiled in part by psychologist Jonathan Haidt. I've summarized that list and added some additional ideas here as well.

- Read the works of great thinkers (e.g., Gandhi, Mother Theresa, Nelson Mandela, Martin Luther King Jr.). Read classic works of literature. Contemplate the "wisdom of the ages."
- Consider a position that is opposite of yours; genuinely try to understand both sides of an issue.
- Think of wise people you've known or have read about. Follow their example in a way that feels authentic for you.
- Volunteer with the elderly and use your strength of curiosity, asking them about the lessons they have learned throughout their lives and what wisdom they would like to share with you.[157]

Remember that wisdom, like any character strength, can be developed with effort and life experience.[158]

CULTIVATING CONDITIONS FOR INSIGHT

Let's now look at the related concept of "insight." Great moments of insight throughout history include Archimedes shouting "Eureka!" when he saw his bathwater rise, and Isaac Newton understanding gravity as an apple fell from a tree. What happens inside the brain to produce insight? Jonah Lehrer wrote about insight in a *New Yorker* article pointing to neuroscientist Mark Jung-Beeman of Northwestern University who studied the insight phenomenon for many years, and mapped the brain's circuitry. Combining EEG with MRI, he found that subjects in a study who solved puzzles using insight activated a specific subset of cortical areas. First, the brain tries to block out distractions, focusing on the problem to be solved, and then it looks for answers. An insight often comes just before the brain is ready to give up, when it finally lets go of the problem and relaxes, spiking the gamma rhythm, which is the highest electrical frequency generated by the brain.[159]

Many conclude that an effective way to produce an insight might be to let the mind wander or take a warm shower (because the relaxation phase is crucial). However, it seems that this works only if you have focused on the solution until you are at an impasse and, ready to give up, you finally relax enough to receive the answer. Insights are one of the secrets of the prefrontal cortex about which we hope to learn more.

Another ideal moment for insights, according to scientists, is the early morning right after we wake up.[160] The drowsy brain is relaxed, unwound, and disorganized, open to all sorts of unconventional ideas. The right hemisphere is also unusually active. Try not to let the morning rush squash your creative insights. Build time in your morning to wake up slowly and simply lie still and think creatively before you have to get out of bed.

Trying to force an insight by over-focusing on a problem can actually prevent the insight. Rather, a holistic, positive, strengths-oriented approach appears to produce better results. Research has demonstrated that making people focus on the details of a visual scene, as opposed to the big picture, can significantly disrupt the insight process.[161] If you work in a stressful, overachieving, overdriving environment and don't build in relaxation breaks to step back and clear your head, you may find your creativity slumping. Many of the most forward-thinking companies, like Google, understand this and provide relaxation activities at work to enable creativity and insight. The data is in—people who are in a good mood are much better at solving puzzles and developing creative solutions.

LIFELONG LEARNING AND CURIOSITY

Doreetha Daniels graduated with her associate degree from College of the Canyons, in Santa Clarita, California. The event may have seemed unremarkable, if not for the fact that Daniels was 99 years old. Daniels stated her reason for getting her degree—she wanted to better herself. After six years of schooling, she earned her degree, along with the profound respect from those who have heard her story. Even Michelangelo reportedly said at age 87: "I am still learning."

How can we become lifelong learners? Not everyone enjoys formal education or has the time and money to pursue it—especially later in life. However, learning isn't limited to formal education, degrees, and institutions. In our current world, we have access to learning on so many platforms—from books and online courses to professional development programs and podcasts, it's easier than ever to make a habit of becoming a lifelong learner. Let's look at some of the benefits of adopting the habits and mindset of a lifelong learner.

- First, learning is good for our health. Reading can lower our stress levels. Engaging in cognitive activities can delay the symptoms of diseases such as Alzheimer's, increasing our quality of life. Learning new skills later in life, such as playing a new instrument, can improve memory and slow cognitive decline.

- Second, curiosity and open-mindedness yield positive benefits. John Coleman, author and contributor to the *Harvard Business Review,* shares the following example: "...I've noticed in my own interactions that those who dedicate themselves to learning and who exhibit curiosity are almost always happier and more socially and professionally engaging than those who don't...Think of the best conversationalist you know. Do they ask good questions? Are they well-informed?"[162]

- Finally, lifelong learning promotes human flourishing. Again, John Coleman writes: "Have you ever sat in a quiet place and finished a great novel in one sitting? Do you remember the fulfillment you felt when you last settled into a difficult task—whether a math problem or a foreign language course—and found yourself making breakthrough progress? Have you ever worked with a team of friends or colleagues to master difficult material or create something new? These experiences can be electrifying. And even if education had no impact on health, prosperity, or social standing, it would be entirely worthwhile as an expression of what makes every person so special and unique."[163]

The reasons to embrace lifelong learning are innumerable. By implementing this habit and mindset, our lives can improve socially, emotionally, and physically.

RECHARGE YOUR MIND WITH STRENGTHS

Let's explore how we can recharge the mind. Here are three possible ways to do so by using your character strengths. There are myriad other ways to employ your character strengths to make your mind healthy and expansive.

JUDGMENT	CURIOSITY	LOVE OF LEARNING
Judgment is also called open-mindedness. Expand your mind by trying to understand others.	Spend five minutes each day observing everything around you using all five senses. Record your observations.	Choose a topic you know little about and research it.

EXERCISE: MIND

Let's do a fun exercise to enliven and expand the mind.

- **Step 1:** Find a partner. As a pair, plan an outing. Partner A will start by sharing an idea. Partner B will respond with the words "Yes, but..." and a reason why the idea will not work—blocking that person's idea. Then, Partner B will share an idea and Partner A will respond with "Yes, but..." and a reason why this idea will not work—again, blocking the other person's idea. Continue doing this back and forth for a few minutes.

- **Step 2:** Continue to work with your same partner. You are still tasked with planning an outing. As partners, you will continue to share back and forth. But this time, instead of saying "Yes, but..." change it to "Yes, and..." accepting your partner's idea and building on it. Continue doing this back and forth for a few minutes.

Take a moment to answer the following questions about your experience in your *Well-Being Workbook*:

- What was the difference between blocking another person's idea and accepting an idea while adding to it?
- What are the benefits and costs of: "Yes, but..." vs. "Yes, and..."?
- What is the impact of blocking vs. accepting on any creative process with other people?

MIND: MINDFULNESS PRACTICE

Let's end our discussion about the mind with a mindfulness practice. Again, you can read this practice and experience it in its written form below, or you can listen to the mindfulness practices at AuthenticStrengths.com:

Move your attention to the center area of your forehead.
Imagine that this corresponds to your open-mindedness, reasoning, imagination, wisdom, insight, and life-long learning.
Envision your mind expanding as you listen to your highest and best self—your inner coach.
Recharge as you say: I am a wise, imaginative, intuitive, rational, lifelong learner, my mind is clear and healthy.
Take a moment to savor the positive responses this awakens within you.

SPIRIT

CHAPTER SEVEN

SPIRIT

"Never underestimate the power of dreams
and the influence of the human spirit."[164]

—WILMA RUDOLPH

YOUR SPIRIT

The final element we will explore in this book is that of spirit. Our character strengths are intricately linked to our spirit—to what we could call our "spiritual DNA."

A five-year old boy named Koby, wise beyond his years, described how our character strengths elevate our spirit. Koby simply said, "Character strengths are the keys to your heart that make your spirit rise and allow you to do things better."[165] Our character strengths are in essence our potential—the highest expression of our humanness. They are that part of us where human virtue and goodness resides. We could consider our character strengths as our "spiritual DNA" because collectively our character strengths give meaning and purpose to our lives, enabling our spirits to soar.

I use the words "spiritual DNA" here not in a religious sense, although it can certainly be that for many people, but to describe the inner worth and potential that each of us carries within. This inherent worth and potential characterizes the resilient, unconquerable human spirit—our highest, best, and virtuous self. Additionally, research findings on the benefits of the strength of spirituality, as summarized on the VIA website, found that spirituality "provides a sense of being grounded, increases optimism, and helps provide a sense of purpose for life.

These in turn contribute to an overall sense of well-being. Youth who describe themselves as spiritual show better self-regulation and academic performance and tend to see the world as a more coherent place. Spirituality has also been linked to many character strengths, including humility, forgiveness, gratitude, kindness, hope, love and zest."[166]

Many studies show that people who practice some form of spirituality are happier.[167] Spirituality can involve committing to a life of integrity to our values, listening to inspirational and uplifting music, serving in our community, or practicing spiritual worship that edifies. One of the key components of spirituality is feeling positive emotions that connect you to something greater than yourself.

It's interesting to note that in Oprah Winfrey's work, and in her words below she reveals her reverence for honoring the human spirit, as well as her innate desire to connect to something greater than self: "I want to illuminate the possibility of the human spirit."[168] Further, I would personally add that the deepest need of the human spirit is to have one's authenticity be seen. When I watch Oprah interview people, I find her brilliance in putting people at ease is in seeing, and in reflecting back to them their best self. She is fully present with those she interviews.

Connecting to your strengths is a spiritual renewal in and of itself. In fact, using your strengths to recharge any of the many facets of your being will make the process much more enjoyable and meaningful!

SPIRIT: CREATING A POSITIVE MINDSET

Let's check in with our mindset in this element of the spirit to see if we are listening more to our inner critic or to our inner coach. If we want to rise to our potential, we must learn to turn down the noise of the inner critic that can ring so loudly in our ears, and to go inward instead. One way to do this is by regularly stilling ourselves long enough to reconnect with our higher self. It's through that inward journey that we can hear the voice of our spirit—our inner coach.

In this final mindset check for the spirit, once again, place a mark where you are currently on the arrow continuum for each statement about the spirit mindset. Next, consider where you want to be over time.

INNER CRITIC	VS.	INNER COACH
Apathy	←——————→	Meaning/Purpose
Hopelessness	←——————→	Hopeful
Unappreciative	←——————→	Grateful
Serve Self Only	←——————→	Serve Self and Others
Distracted	←——————→	Present Awareness

Inner Coach vs. Inner Critic Model: Spirit, © 2014-2021,
Authentic Strengths Advantage, LLC. All rights reserved.

SPIRIT: THE CORE FOUR

Here are the core four principles for the spirit. They are:

- **Meaning/Purpose:** We endeavor to understand the "why" of life and connect it to a greater whole.
- **Hope/Gratitude:** Using the strengths of hope and gratitude we increase our overall sense of well-being.
- **Awe/Wonder:** These are positive feelings that transcend our understanding of the world.
- **Inward Journey:** Here we find synergy between mindful living and character strengths.

Next, let's get started with the first of the core four for the spirit element: meaning and purpose...

MEANING AND PURPOSE

The first core principle of the spirit element is "meaning/purpose." The character strength of spirituality has been defined as the ability to see one's place in the scheme of the universe (or the outer world) and thus to find meaning and purpose in everyday life. Spirituality has also been defined by scientists on the VIA website as "the search for, or connection with 'the sacred.'" They continue: "The sacred might be that which is blessed, holy, revered or particularly special... sacredness might be pursued as the search for a purpose in life or as a close relationship with something greater; the sacred might be experienced in the forgiveness offered by a child, a humble moment between a leader and a subordinate, an awe-inspiring sunset, a profound experience during meditation or a religious service, or the self-sacrificing kindness of a stranger. As a character strength, spirituality involves the belief that there is a dimension to life that is beyond human understanding."[169]

So, as we approach this core principle of meaning and purpose from a well-being perspective, Mark Hyman, MD reminds us with this strong assertion: "...meaning, purpose and connection in life is one of the most powerful factors that determine our health and well-being."[170]

YOUR "I AM" MOTIVATION

I've witnessed many breakthroughs when people come to understand the "why" behind their actions. It comes down to motivation. For example, consider what truly motivates you when you ask yourself what is your source of meaning and purpose? What are your "I am" beliefs? Are they empowering you with sustainable sources of intrinsic motivation, or are you motivated by unsustainable sources outside of yourself? Understanding this can be a game changer. Choosing "I am" strengths motivation will provide you with authentic, sustainable motivation that gets you the most effective results. It's less about what you do and more about *why* you do what you do—your belief systems about yourself and the world.

When you consider the words "I am," what comes to the forefront for you? How do you see your highest and best self? How can you consistently use your language to support this vision of your highest and best self? What language and thoughts will you be more conscious of going forward as you actualize this new vision of yourself? How can you empower this higher vision of yourself using your character strengths? The answers require introspection and the courage to shape your own future by designing your life instead of passively letting it be determined for you. The result will be a powerful sense of meaning and purpose.

My friend, Nathan Osmond, shared the story below about his epiphany in using the words "I am":

My brothers and I, The Osmonds 2nd Generation, starred in the North American Tour of the classic musical, *You're A Good Man Charlie Brown*. I was cast in the lead role of "Charlie Brown." When receiving the good news, I decided right there and then that I would be the best Charlie Brown this world had ever seen!

I immediately went to a local store and purchased a Charlie Brown t-shirt. You know the one...yellow with the classic black zig-zag design around the midsection. I next went to the Hallmark store and asked if I could purchase the Charlie Brown cardboard cut-out they had in their display window. While trying to purchase it, Charles Schultz' granddaughter, entered the store and argued that she deserved to have it as her grandfather was the one who created the character. The store ended up selling it to me. I put that red flannel Charlie Brown cutout with the hunter's hat in my apartment where I could look at him every single day.

My girlfriend's parents purchased me a book full of Charlie Brown comics so that I could really get familiar with the character. I would walk around the room with a brown paper bag over my head. I would look in the mirror and say to myself, "good grief" and other Charlie Brownisms. I was gonna be the absolute spitting image of this character!

I made it my mission to channel my inner-Charlie Brown. One particular scene that I worked on was called, "The Doctor Is In" where Lucy says to Charlie Brown, "I think what you need most of all Charlie Brown, is to come right out and admit all the things that are wrong with you." Charlie Brown then begins to sing a song. Here are some of the words to that song:

"I'm not very handsome, or clever, or lucid,
I've always been stupid at spelling and numbers.
I've never been much playing football or baseball

Or stickball, or checkers, or marbles, or ping-pong
I'm usually awful at parties and dances,
I stand like a stick or I cough, or I laugh,
Or I don't bring a present, or I spill the ice cream
Or I get so depressed that I stand and I scream...
Oh, how could there possibly be
One small person as thoroughly, totally, utterly
Blah as me.

Those casting directors were spot on...That character was becoming me! I was failing my math class. I began struggling in certain social situations. I lacked self-confidence. And worst of all, I was carrying around a heaviness on my shoulders and chest that seemed to weigh me down. It made no sense at all! If you know me, you know that I am an upbeat guy. Then why all the heaviness? I knew I needed to find a quiet place where I could be still and think. I needed a place where I could meditate on my current situation and find some answers. So, I drove my car to a special place and parked it. As I sat in my car trying to figure myself out, it was as if someone sitting in the passenger seat of that car spoke to me out loud and said, "Why don't you start loving yourself the way that I love you?"

It was so clear as day that I actually looked to the passenger seat as if someone from that seat had just said those words to me. Although I didn't see anyone sitting there, I knew who had just spoken to me. It was in that moment that I came to the realization that I had literally become Charlie Brown. I realized right there that I had become my own worst enemy. I was beating myself up and ripping myself to shreds each and every day as I put on that yellow shirt and put that brown paper bag over my head. I began manifesting everything I sang in that song. If you notice, the words "I Am" are at the front of nearly every one of those lines. I realized that if God could love me with all my bumps and scrapes and imperfections, then why couldn't I love myself? I went and bought myself a milkshake and started finding a friend in the mirror.

Many an actor has met their fate in this business because they commit to becoming a certain character. Angelina Jolie has talked quite a bit about how hard it's been for her to break out of certain characters. It can really mess with your mind. What took Heath Ledger's life? It was "The Joker." He committed himself to that role to the extent that he couldn't get out of it. What a tragic ending to a very talented young man's life!

Now that I'm a father, I tell my four sons to be careful what they tell themselves because they might actually believe it. When I speak publicly, I ask the question, "By a show of hands, how many of you talk to yourselves?" I see most hands go up. I then follow that question by saying, "Those of you who aren't raising your hands right now are saying, 'I don't know, do I talk to myself?' Ha! We ALL do it!" Sometimes the most riveting conversations you are ever going to have are the ones that you have with yourself. Sometimes the only nice thing you're ever going to hear are the things that YOU say to YOU, so be GOOD to YOU!! And learn to be lighthearted with yourself.

I recently spoke to my uncle Donny Osmond. As he walked me out to my car, he gave me some very powerful advice. He said, "Nathan, sometimes in life we live in the extremes. It's either all white or all black. Here's my advice: be ok to live in the gray." In other words, find a happy medium. Be sure to pat yourself on the back every once in a while and give yourself credit for your efforts. Don't wallow—take time to find that friend in the mirror. You are priceless beyond words.

HOPE AND GRATITUDE.

The next core principle is "hope/gratitude." Both hope and gratitude are ways of thinking that manifest joy in our lives. In the words of David Steindl-Rast: "The root of joy is gratefulness. It's not joy that makes us grateful, it's gratitude that makes us joyful."[171] So, how important are positive thoughts and emotions such as hope and gratitude in influencing the experiences of our lives?

Research reveals that when we are in a negative state, experiencing fear, anger, and discouragement, our ability to solve problems decreases significantly. We literally take in less information, see fewer options to solving problems, and remember less. We have less patience and are more irritable, thereby straining relationships and decreasing our ability to influence situations. In sharp contrast, when we focus on the positive, such as considering all that we are hopeful or grateful for, we have more positive thoughts, eliciting positive emotions. Our feelings of faith, hope, and optimism grow. Researcher Barbara Fredrickson calls this effect "broaden and build," which basically means that our problem-solving ability and intelligence literally increase after immersion in positive and enriching influences. Study subjects exposed to positive influences, such as uplifting films, music, poetry, etc., consistently and significantly outperformed their study counterparts who had been exposed to negativity.[172]

While I was teaching a workshop, a participant approached me during the break to share her experience using her strengths of hope and gratitude. In her words below:

My family fled Iran due to economic hardships and our search for religious freedom. We traveled to Pakistan and became refugees for two and a half years in very terrible conditions, enduring tremendous stress. After being approved for immigration, I felt so grateful that we were able to arrive safely in the U.S. and made myself a promise to try my best to use my strengths of hope and gratitude in any situation.

I was tempted to think negatively, however, when I was laid off from work, nearly spiraling down into despair. In the stress, I had given up trying to stay positive and I was feeling very sorry for myself. Every Monday morning when I would get up to search for work, I would see on Facebook many of my friends talking about how they despised Mondays because they would have to go to work at the start of a new week. And here I was looking for work every day and trying for months to find a job! That is when I was reminded of my commitment to use my hope and gratitude, and I resolved to never complain about going to work on Mondays when I finally found a job.

I did finally land a job and feel grateful that I have the strength and health to get up in the morning and have the opportunity to go to work. Now each Monday I'm happy to start my day. I say a prayer in my car as I'm driving to work. When I get to work, I greet everyone by saying Happy Monday! I do definitely get looks as people remind me in bewilderment that it's Monday, surprised that I could be happy about returning from my weekend. My answer to them is that I'm healthy and I have a job—therefore I'm grateful for Mondays.

As you saw in the story above, gratitude and hope are character strengths that induce positivity, helping to dispel discouragement, despair, and negativity.[173] Let's focus on building these strengths by doing the following exercises.

EXERCISE: HOPE

Think of one thing you are optimistic and hopeful about right now. Then, using colored markers or pencils, choose a color and write your answer down, or draw something representative on a piece of paper. Next, using a different color, write or draw a second thing, and then a third, and so on, until the paper is filled up with interesting colors representing many of your hopes and aspirations. Post it somewhere you will see it for the next week. Your goal is to create a beautiful, colorful depiction of hope that will inspire you whenever you look at it. This will remind you to be more optimistic and hopeful.

Next, answer the following questions in your *Well-Being Workbook*:

- How did it feel to do this hope exercise?
- What insights did you gain?
- How will you keep your hope and optimism alive going forward?

EXERCISE: GRATITUDE

Expressing gratitude for the character strengths in others has many benefits, such as improving your relationships and bringing more joy into your life and the lives of others. Take some time to do the following exercise:

- Spend the next five minutes writing a note or sending a text to someone in your life to whom you are grateful for their use of their character strengths.
- Be as descriptive in this gratitude note as you can—identifying the character strengths you have noticed them use and how those character strengths have benefited you and others. Hand this note or send this text to that person.
- Write about your insights from doing this gratitude exercise in your *Well-Being Workbook* and how you will continue to cultivate more gratitude in your life.

AWE AND WONDER

Researchers have created a description of awe and wonder as follows: "that sense of wonder we feel in the presence of something vast that transcends our understanding of the world."[174] People most often experience feelings of awe and wonder while in nature, but also experience them in response to other things, such as music, art, spirituality, and experiences that touch and lift their spirit within. Marcus Aurelius poetically described the feelings of awe and wonder as: "Dwell on the beauty of life. Watch the stars, and see yourself running with them."[175]

Some scientists have increased their focus on studying the experience of awe and wonder in just the past couple of decades. Awe and wonder are emotions that are multi-faceted and difficult to define. They are something we can feel when staring out onto a great vista, listening to beautiful music, or reading something that resonates with our higher self—our spirit. We can experience awe and wonder from a well-told story or profound movie plot. We can experience these emotions while standing in front of a majestic structure like the Notre Dame. Or we can feel them when at a concert, during a dance performance, or even when witnessing an incredible act of courage.

Different experiences and things can induce awe and wonder in each of us. An expanding amount of research points to a significant range of positive benefits, including an increase in physical and mental well-being, and a strengthening of our generosity, humility, and perspective.[176]

Experiencing awe and wonder in our lives may be more important than we realize. The following study was summarized in an article from the Greater Good Science Center: "In a recent study, researchers took military veterans and youth from underserved communities whitewater rafting. They found that the more awe the participants experienced, the more improvement they saw in their well-being and symptoms of stress one week later. According to a different survey the researchers conducted, undergraduate students reported greater life satisfaction and well-being on days when they spent time in nature, which was attributable to the higher level of awe they felt on those days. This suggests that awe just might be a crucial ingredient in nature's restorative powers."

The researchers went on to state: "People in awe start to appreciate their sense of selfhood as less separate and more interrelated to the larger existence. The experience of awe elevates people from their mundane concerns, which are bounded by daily experiences such as the desire for money."[177]

THE INWARD JOURNEY

The final core principle for the element of spirit is the "inward journey." Research has shown the benefit of infusing character strengths with mindfulness and meditation, which are methods of accessing our inward journey. Dr. Ryan Niemiec, VIA Institute on Character Education Director, concludes from his recent studies: "There is a powerful, albeit hypothetical, synergy between character strengths and approaches to mindful living, such as mindful eating, driving, working, walking, speaking, and listening, in which each mutually enhances the other and creates opportunities for personal transformation."[178]

The inward journey is a very personal journey, and one size does not fit all. Mindfulness doesn't have to be equated with monks in a faraway monastery, living an austere life outside of mainstream society. Although this can be compelling for some, others want a practical, easy-to-apply approach to access their inward journey. Embarking on the inward journey can be as simple as sitting quietly and breathing deeply to calm the body and mind. When we are in this state, we are more receptive to the whisperings of our inner coach. And when we ponder or meditate on our character strengths during these peaceful moments of quiet and introspection, we are more likely to feel uplifted and inspired to be our best self.

As Dr. Niemiec has said: "To merge character strengths and mindfulness is to bring a deep awareness to our best qualities and to use these abilities to improve our awareness of all aspects of our lives. Mindfulness and character strengths deepen one another. To practice using character strengths with mindfulness is to be intentional and conscious about noticing and deploying your best qualities."[179]

RECHARGE YOUR SPIRIT WITH STRENGTHS

Let's now consider how you can recharge your spirit with just a few ideas to jump start your thinking.

SPIRITUALITY	APPRECIATION OF BEAUTY & EXCELLENCE	HOPE
Engage in a mindfulness practice, prayer, or meaningful moment enjoying nature's majesty.	Appreciate with awe & wonder the immensity of the night sky or a beautiful place in nature.	Focus on the positive as you look for meaning and purpose in life's difficult moments.

SPIRIT: MINDFULNESS PRACTICE

Let's end our exploration of the spirit element with a mindfulness practice. You can either internalize the written words below, or listen to this mindfulness practice at <u>AuthenticStrengths.com</u>:

Move your attention to the area above the crown of your head.
Imagine that this corresponds to a sense of meaning, purpose, awe, and wonder,
a connection to something greater than self.
Envision being filled with light from the top of your head to the tips of your toes,
feeling deep inner gratitude.
Recharge by saying, "My life has meaning and purpose. I am grateful, hopeful,
and filled with awe at the miracle of life.
Take a moment to bathe in the positive emotions that arise within you.

AFTERWORD

WELL-BEING IS YOUR TRUE NATURE

As you come to the close of this book, have you begun to experience revitalized energy in each of the seven elements we have explored? Have you benefited from your newly developed awareness? Your well-being and energy are interrelated. Neglecting one key area of your overall self can throw everything else off balance. Your success enlivening and enhancing your well-being depends upon addressing the many related aspects of your life—paying attention to the integrated systems that impact your ability to flourish. The benefits of doing so are exponential.

Making the commitment to consistently recharge the multiple facets of your being is supported by shifting from "no" to "yes." Saying yes to cultivating your well-being and to what you aspire can be more compelling than saying no to the lifestyle choices you are trying to avoid. It's a shift from exhausting negatives to energizing affirmatives. When you learn to focus on what you want instead of what you don't want, that positive shift taps into your motivating, energizing, deeper yes! The heartening words of Bruce H. Lipton, PhD give life to this deeper yes rooted in your strengths of character: "I was exhilarated by the new realization that I could change the character of my life...I was instantly energized because I realized there was a science-based path that would take me from my job as a perennial 'victim' to my new position as 'co-creator' of my destiny."[180]

Do you say yes to the simple things in life that invigorate your well-being, or do you miss those sometimes mundane, yet sacred moments of self-renewal? Consider a sunrise: to someone who sees it solely from a mechanical viewpoint, it's merely light refracted into multiple colors. However, when you place your attention upon it using your character strengths, such as appreciation of beauty, gratitude, love, or hope, it's alchemized into something that induces well-being. You may literally feel it expanding your heart with feel-good endorphins, as it lifts your mood. So, you hold your well-being within your own hands, influencing your day-to-day experiences with where you choose to place your awareness.

Any gardener knows that what one nourishes grows more vibrant and stronger, prevailing like the undeterred plants we have all seen emerge through cracks in concrete. What do you choose to nourish—the flowers or the weeds?

Take out your *Well-Being Workbook* one last time and reflect on the most valuable insights you've gained.

- What are you already doing well and where can you continue to grow?
- What are the commitments you will make to continuously improve your own well-being going forward?

Write your insights and commitments down in your workbook as an act of self-love and self-affirmation that will germinate what you truly want in your life.

I'd like to close with a beautiful description of our true nature—our innate well-being that lies within—rooted in embracing the best within us and in saying "yes" to life. It's my hope that the quote below lingers with you well beyond you closing the cover of this book. It comes from author and teacher, Mooji:

> Love is our nature, peace and joy and an appreciation of what is right and what is good. These are the qualities, the perfume of our true nature...Fear comes because we have moved away from our central nature...now is a beautiful opportunity to wake up, to discover what is real about us, what is true...[181]

I wish you great success in your quest to elevate your well-being, and I encourage you to help those you care about to do the same! Enjoy the journey!

ACKNOWLEDGEMENTS

It's with heartfelt thanks that I acknowledge the many people who have helped make this book possible. I am deeply grateful to my husband Rob and my sons Kaden and Sage for their unconditional love and encouragement. Words cannot express how much I love and adore them, and my heart is full with the joy they bring into my life daily.

To my parents, Tiberio and Isabel Silveira, for the courage, perseverance, and hope they exercised when faced with uncommon challenges. They left behind their country of birth in order to provide greater opportunities and a better life for our family. I love them and will always be humbled by and grateful for their selfless contributions.

To my siblings, with much love and with whom I have created many joyful memories—you have always supported my work and my dreams. We have comforted each other through life's difficulties, and I am grateful for the beautiful bond we share.

To Dr. Neal H. Mayerson, and Dr. Donna Mayerson, whose service to the cause of strengths education is helping to build a better world. I greatly appreciate your dedication to the mission of the VIA Institute on Character. To Dr. Ryan Niemiec, Breta Cooper, Kelly Alluise, and Chris Jenkins at the VIA Institute on Character, who work diligently to spread the empowering message of character strengths to the world.

To Tiffany Yoast, my incredibly gifted friend and colleague, who helped me as a sounding board while I discussed my new ideas, tools, and theories with her, and who helped with some research and in the graphic design process.

To Dr. Martin E.P. Seligman, whose groundbreaking work in the field of positive psychology and hopeful message to the world inspired me to write this book.

To my friends and colleagues, David Covey and Stephan Mardyks, whose work at SMCOVEY helping authors to share empowering content is increasing fulfillment for many by improving the way people live, work, and do business around the world.

To my alma mater, the Columbia University Coaching Certification Program, and to my friend and colleague, Dr. Terry Maltbia, who continues to inspire me to make a positive difference through my coaching work.

To Heather Moon, who verified research citations and was a reader of the manuscript.

To Matthew Morse, who did the beautiful cover design and interior layout of this book. Images by: Deposit Photos/Markin, Shutterstock/Paket; Shutterstock/Beautiful Landscape; Shutterstock/Artens; Pexels/Neale LaSalle; Pixabay/cafepampas; Pexels/Pixabay; and hotshotworldwide.

I am grateful to the many people who supported me through their reading of the manuscript and by providing their helpful feedback/edits, namely: Dr. Michael Hunter, Dr. Felicia Alley English, Isabel Silveira Pierce, Chris McLaws, Laurinda Raquel, Darlene Batatian, Raylene Gull, Sue Fendler, Tiffany Yoast, and Megan Heward.

ENDNOTES

1   "Wholeness." Dictionary. Accessed June 22, 2020. https://dictionary.com/Wholeness.

2   "Wholeness." Oxford Learner's Dictionaries. Accessed June 22, 2020. https://www.oxfordlearnersdictionaries.com/us/definition/english/wholeness.

3   "Well-being." Oxford Learner's Dictionaries. Accessed June 22, 2020. https://www.oxfordlearnersdictionaries.com/us/definition/english/well-being.

4   "Well-being." *Wikipedia*. Accessed June 22, 2020. https://en.wikipedia.org/wiki/Well-being.

5   "Well-being." *Wikipedia*. Accessed June 22, 2020. https://en.wikipedia.org/wiki/Well-being.

6   "Constitiution." World Health Organization. Accessed June 22, 2020. https://www.who.int/about/who-we-are/constitution .

7   Levy, Becca R., Martin D. Slade, Suzanne R. Kunkel, and Stanislav V. Kasl. 2002. "Longevity Increased by Positive Self-Perceptions of Aging." *Journal of Personality and Social Psychology* 83 (2): 261–70. https://doi.org/10.1037/0022-3514.83.2.261; Lee, Lewina O., Peter James, Emily S. Zevon, Eric S. Kim, Claudia Trudel-Fitzgerald, Avron Spiro, Francine Grodstein, and Laura D. Kubzansky. 2019. "Optimism Is Associated with Exceptional Longevity in 2 Epidemiologic Cohorts of Men and Women." *Proceedings of the National Academy of Sciences* 116 (37): 18357–62. https://doi.org/10.1073/pnas.1900712116.

8   Pang, D., & Ruch, W. 2019. "Fusing Character Strengths and Mindfulness Interventions: Benefits for Job Satisfaction and Performance." *Journal of Occupational Health Psychology* 24(1): 150-162. http://dx.doi.org/10.1037/ocp0000144.

9   Seligman, M. E. P. *Authentic Happiness: Using the New Positive Psychology to Realize Your Potential for Lasting Fulfillment*. New York: Free Press, 2004;

Seligman, M. E. P. *Flourish: A Visionary New Understanding of Happiness and Well-being*. New York, NY: Free Press, 2011.

10 Marjorie Aunos PhD, email communications beginning November 6, 2020.

11 "What the Research Says About Character Strengths." VIA Institute on Character. Accessed June 22, 2020. https://www.viacharacter.org/research/findings.

12 "What the Research Says About Character Strengths." Via Institute on Character. Accessed June 22, 2020. https://www.viacharacter.org/research/findings.

13 Seifert, Tricia A. "The Ryff Scales of Psychological Well-Being." Center of Inquiry. 2005. Accessed October 3, 2020. https://centerofinquiry.org/uncategorized/ryff-scales-of-psychological-well-being/; "Well-being." *Wikipedia*. Accessed June 22, 2020. https://en.wikipedia.org/wiki/Well-being

14 "Character Strengths and Health and Wellness." VIA Institute on Character. Accessed October 3, 2020. https://www.viacharacter.org/research/findings/character-strengths-and-health-and-wellness.

15 "The VIA Character Strengths Survey." VIA Institute on Character. Accessed October 3, 2020. https://www.viacharacter.org/survey/account/register.

16 Allmendinger, Jutta, Hackman, J. Richard, and Lehman, Erin V. 1996. "Life and Work in Symphony Orchestras." *The Musical Quarterly* 80 (2): 194–219. https://doi.org/10.1093/mq/80.2.194.

17 Neff, Kristen. "The Motivational Power of Self-Compassion." Self-Compassion. 2016. Accessed October 4, 2020. http://self-compassion.org/the-motivational-power-of-self-compassion/.

18 Achor, Shawn, and Michelle Gielan. "Resilience Is About How You Recharge, Not How You Endure." *Harvard Business Review*, June 24, 2016. https://hbr.org/2016/06/resilience-is-about-how-you-recharge-not-how-you-endure.

19 Achor, Shawn, and Michelle Gielan. "Resilience Is About How You Recharge, Not How You Endure." *Harvard Business Review*, June 24, 2016. https://hbr.org/2016/06/resilience-is-about-how-you-recharge-not-how-you-endure.

20 Loehr, Jim, and Tony Schwartz. *The Power of Full Engagement: Managing Energy, Not Time, Is the Key to High Performance and Personal Renewal*. Concordville, Pa.; Norwood, Mass.: Free Press, 2003.

21   Achor, Shawn, and Michelle Gielan. "Resilience Is About How You Recharge, Not How You Endure." *Harvard Business Review*, June 24, 2016. https://hbr. org/2016/06/resilience-is-about-how-you-recharge-not-how-you-endure.

22   Lipton, Bruce H., *The Biology of Belief: Unleashing the Power of Consciousness, Matter, & Miracles*. Carlsbad: Hay House, 2008.

23   Hyman, Mark. "Thoughts are Things." *Our Berkshire Times Magazine*. April 1, 2009. https://www.ourberkshiretimes.com/articles--illustration-blog/ thoughts-are-things-by-dr-mark-hyman-ultrawellness-center.

24   Singer, Michael A., *The Untethered Soul: The Journey Beyond Yourself*. New Harbinger Publications, Inc., 2007.

25   Wisneski, Len, and Lucy Anderson. 2005. "The Scientific Basis of Integrative Medicine." *Evidence-based Complementary and Alternative Medicine*, 2(2), 257–259. https://doi.org/10.1093/ecam/neh079.

26   Harvard Medical School Center for Primary Care. "Mindfulness Can Improve Mental Health During and After the COVID 19 Crisis." Harvard Medical School. July 10, 2020. Accessed April 14, 2021. http://info.primarycare.hms. harvard.edu/blog/mindfulness-during-after-covid.

27   Fallon, Brian. "Can Meditation and Yoga Help Reduce Anxiety Related toCOVID-19? A Study at Columbia University Seeks to Address Heightened Stress During the Pandemic." *Columbia News*. January 28, 2021. Accessed April 14, 2021. https://news.columbia.edu/news/can-meditation-and-yo- ga-help-reduce-anxiety-related-covid-19.

28   Student Voices. "Alternative Medicine for Your Health." Columbia Public Health. July 22, 2015. Accessed April 14, 2021. https://www.publichealth. columbia.edu/public-health-now/news/alternative-medicine-your-health.

29   Heijer, Alexander den. *Nothing You Don't Already Know: Remarkable Remind- ers about Meaning, Purpose, and Self-Realization*. Scotts Valley, CA: Cre- ateSpace Independent Publishing Platforms, 2018.

30   "What Impact Does the Environment Have on Us?" Taking Charge of Your Health & Wellbeing. University of Minnesota. Accessed October 4, 2020. https://www.takingcharge.csh.umn.edu/what-impact-does-environment- have-us.

31   "How Does Your Personal Environment Impact Your Wellbeing?" Taking Charge of Your Health & Wellbeing. University of Minnesota. Accessed October 4, 2020. https://www.takingcharge.csh.umn.edu/enhance-your-wellbeing/environment/your-personal-environment/how-does-your-personal-environment-impa.

32   Ryan, Richard M., Netta Weinstein, Jessey Bernstein, Kirk Warren Brown, Louis Mistretta, and Marylène Gagné. 2010. "Vitalizing Effects of Being Outdoors and in Nature." *Journal of Environmental Psychology* 30 (2): 159–68. https://doi.org/10.1016/j.jenvp.2009.10.009.

33   Beam. Accessed October 4, 2020. https://beam.org

34   Eco-Age Staff. "15 Inspiring People Changing the World Today." Eco-Age. November 29, 2019. Accessed October 4, 2020. https://eco-age.com/magazine/inspiring-people-changing-the-world/.

35   Eco-Age Staff. "15 Inspiring People Changing the World Today." Eco-Age. November 29, 2019. Accessed October 4, 2020. https://eco-age.com/magazine/inspiring-people-changing-the-world/.

36   Hall, Karyn. "Create a Sense of Belonging." *Psychology Today*. March 24, 2014. Accessed November 29, 2019. https://www.psychologytoday.com/us/blog/pieces-mind/201403/create-sense-belonging.

37   Hearne, Kevin. *Shattered*. New York: Del Rey, 2014; Hall, Karyn. "Create a Sense of Belonging." *Psychology Today*. March 24, 2014. Accessed November 29, 2019. https://www.psychologytoday.com/us/blog/pieces-mind/201403/create-sense-belonging.

38   "Refuge." Oxford Learner's Dictionaries. Accessed June 22, 2020. https://www.oxfordlearnersdictionaries.com/us/definition/english/refuge.

39   Rinpoche, Youngey Mingyur. "Why We Take Refuge." Lion's Roar. March 20, 2018. Accessed October 4, 2020. https://www.lionsroar.com/why-we-take-refuge/.

40   "Sanctuary." Oxford Learner's Dictionaries. Accessed June 22, 2020. https://www.oxfordlearnersdictionaries.com/us/definition/english/sanctuary.

41   Finding Sanctuary. Accessed October 4, 2020. https://findingsanctuary.com/.

42   Barrington-Leigh, Chris. "Sustainability and Well-Being: A Happy Synergy." Great Transition Initiative. April 2017. Accessed October 4, 2020. https://greattransition.org/publication/sustainability-and-well-being.

43   Ryback, Ralph. "The Powerful Psychology Behind Cleanliness." *Psychology Today*. July 11, 2016. Accessed October 4, 2020. https://www.psychologytoday.com/us/blog/the-truisms-wellness/201607/the-powerful-psychology-behind-cleanliness.

44   Francis, Meagan. "About Meagan." Meagan Francis. Accessed June 26, 2020. http://meaganfrancis.com/about/.

45   "How Does Your Personal Environment Impact Your Wellbeing?" Taking Charge of Your Health & Wellbeing. University of Minnesota. Accessed October 4, 2020. https://www.takingcharge.csh.umn.edu/enhance-your-wellbeing/environment/your-personal-environment/how-does-your-personal-environment-impa.

46   Lino, Catarina. "Broaden-and-Build Theory of Positive Emotions (+PDF)." Positive Psychology. January 9, 2020. Accessed June 26, 2020. https://positivepsychology.com/broaden-build-theory/.

47   Cohen, Aren. "Comfort Has Many Facets." Positive Psychology. October 16, 2013. Accessed October 4, 2020. https://positivepsychologynews.com/news/aren-cohen/2013101627436.

48   Cerretani, Jessica. "The Contagion of Happiness." *Harvard Medicine*. Spring 2021. Accessed May 17, 2021. https://hms.harvard.edu/magazine/science-emotion/contagion-happiness.

49   Fredrickson Barbara L. 2004. "The Broaden–and–Build Theory of Positive Emotions." *Philosophical Transactions of the Royal Society of London. Series B: Biological Sciences* 359 (1449): 1367–77. https://doi.org/10.1098/rstb.2004.1512.

50   Tal Ben-Shahar. *Choose the Life You Want: The Mindful Way to Happiness.* Chapel Hill, NC: Algonquin Books, 2014.

51   "Positive Psychology. "Harvard Medical School: Harvard Health. Accessed October 4, 2020. https://www.health.harvard.edu/topics/positive-psychology.

52   "Mindfulness." *Wikipedia*. Accessed June 26, 2020. https://en.wikipedia.org/wiki/Mindfulness.

53 McDonough, Megan. "Defining Embodied Positive Psychology." Whole Being Institute. Accessed October 4, 2020. https://wholebeinginstitute.com/defining-embodied-positive-psychology/.

54 McDonough, Megan. "Defining Embodied Positive Psychology." Whole Being Institute. Accessed October 4, 2020. https://wholebeinginstitute.com/defining-embodied-positive-psychology/.

55 "Wayne Dyer." Brainy Quote. Accessed Oct 3, 2020. https://www.brainyquote.com/quotes/wayne_dyer_154383.

56 Rozin, Paul, and Edward B. Royzman. 2001. "Negativity Bias, Negativity Dominance, and Contagion." *Personality and Social Psychology Review* 5 (4): 296–320. https://doi.org/10.1207/S15327957PSPR0504_2.

57 Wayne Dyer." Brainy Quote. Accessed Oct 3, 2020. https://www.brainyquote.com/quotes/wayne_dyer_154383.

58 "Prosperity." Merriam-Webster. Accessed October 4, 2020. https://www.merriam-webster.com/dictionary/prosperity?src=search-dict-box.

59 Gielan, Michelle. "The Financial Upside of Being an Optimist." *Harvard Business Review*. March 12, 2019. https://hbr.org/2019/03/the-financial-upside-of-being-an-optimist.

60 "Anthony Robbins." Goodreads. Accessed June 26, 2020. https://www.goodreads.com/quotes/157336-when-you-are-grateful-fear-disappears-and-abundance-appears.

61 Emmons, Robert. "Why Gratitude is Good." *Greater Good Magazine*. November 16, 2010. Accessed May 10, 2021. https://greatergood.berkeley.edu/article/item/why_gratitude_is_good.

62 Schwartzburg, Louie. *Gratitude Revealed. Moving Art.* 2018. https://moving-art.com/gratitude-revealed/.

63 "Resourceful." Lexico. Accessed October 4, 2020. https://www.lexico.com/definition/resourceful.

64 "Resourceful." Webster Dictionary. Accessed June 26, 2020. https://www.webster-dictionary.org/definition/Resourceful.

65 "Epicurus." Goodreads. Accessed June 26, 2020. https://www.goodreads.com/quotes/165214-not-what-we-have-but-what-we-enjoy-constitutes-our.

66   Whyte, David. *The Heart Aroused: Poetry and the Preservation of the Soul of Corporate America*. New York: Crown Business, 1996.

67   "Savoring." *Wikipedia*. Accessed Oct 3, 2020. https://en.wikipedia.org/wiki/Savoring.

68   Davis, Tchiki. "What Is Savoring—and Why Is It the Key to Happiness?" *Psychology Today*. July 3, 2018. Accessed June 22, 2020. https://www.psychologytoday.com/us/blog/click-here-happiness/201807/what-is-savoring-and-why-is-it-the-key-happiness.

69   Bryant, Fred. *Savoring: A New Model of Positive Experience*. Abingdon: Routledge, 2006.

70   Kubu, Cynthia and Andre Machado. "The Science is Clear: Why Multitasking Doesn't Work." Cleveland Clinic. June 1, 2017. https://health.clevelandclinic.org/science-clear-multitasking-doesnt-work/.

71   "Covey, Stephen R." Inspiring Quotes. Accessed September 1, 2019. https://www.inspiringquotes.us/author/1333-stephen-covey/about-abundance

72   "Mark Twain Quotes." Goodreads. Accessed September 1, 2019. https://www.goodreads.com/quotes/548857-comparison-is-the-death-of-joy.

73   boutje777. "Keeping up with the Joneses." Newspaper Comic Strips (blog). February 20, 2016. https://newspapercomicstripsblog.wordpress.com/2016/02/20/keeping-up-with-the-joneses/.

74   Price, Catherine. "Trapped—The Secret Ways Social Media is Built to be Addictive (and What You Can Do to Fight Back.)" *Science Focus*. October 29, 2018. https://www.sciencefocus.com/future-technology/trapped-the-secret-ways-social-media-is-built-to-be-addictive-and-what-you-can-do-to-fight-back/.

75   Blankson, Amy. *The Future of Happiness: 5 Modern Strategies for Balancing Productivity and Well-Being in the Digital Era*. Dallas: BenBella Books, 2017.

76   Smith, Sara. "5-4-3-2-1 Coping Technique for Anxiety." Behavioral Health Partners. University of Rochester Medical Center. Accessed June 22, 2020. https://www.urmc.rochester.edu/behavioral-health-partners/bhp-blog/april-2018/5-4-3-2-1-coping-technique-for-anxiety.aspx.

77   Berkeley Well-Being Institute. Accessed October 4, 2020. https://www.berkeleywellbeing.com/.

78 Hyman, Mark. *The UltraMind Solution. Fix Your Broken Brain by Healing Your Body First*. New York: Scribner, 2008.

79 Loehr, Jim, and Tony Schwartz. *The Power of Full Engagement: Managing Energy, Not Time, Is the Key to High Performance and Personal Renewal*. Concordville, Pa.; Norwood, Mass.: Free Press, 2003.

80 "Mahatma Gandhi." Brainy Quote. Accessed Oct 3, 2020. https://www.brainyquote.com/quotes/mahatma_gandhi_109078.

81 "Gautama Buddha." Goodreads. Accessed June 26, 2020. https://www.goodreads.com/quotes/7773216-to-keep-the-body-in-good-health-is-a-duty.

82 Steptoe, Andrew, Katie O'Donnell, Ellena Badrick, Meena Kumari, and Michael Marmot. 2008. "Neuroendocrine and Inflammatory Factors Associated with Positive Affect in Healthy Men and Women." *American Journal of Epidemiology* 167 (1): 96-102. Doi: 10.1093/aje/kwm252.

83 Cohen, Sheldon, Denise Janicki-Deverts, Crista N. Crittenden, and Rodlescia S. Sneed. "Personality and Human Immunity." *Oxford Handbook of Psychoneuroimmunology*. New York: Oxford University Press, 2012. 146-169.

84 Benson, Herbert, and William Proctor. *Relaxation Revolution: The Science and Genetics of Mind Body Healing*. New York: Scribner, 2011.

85 Hyman, Mark. *The UltraMind Solution. Fix Your Broken Brain by Healing Your Body First*. New York: Scribner, 2008.

86 Loehr, Jim, and Tony Schwartz. *The Power of Full Engagement: Managing Energy, Not Time, Is the Key to High Performance and Personal Renewal*. Concordville, Pa.; Norwood, Mass.: Free Press, 2003.

87 "Exercise & Fitness." Harvard Medical School: Harvard Health. Accessed October 4, 2020. https://www.health.harvard.edu/topics/exercise-and-fitness.

88 Kubacky, Gretchen. "Active Relaxation." Dr. Gretchen Kubacky. May 1, 2013. http://drgretchenkubacky.com/thriving/active-relaxation/#.XYPOmC5Kipo.

89 Megan McDonough, discussion with author, November 6, 2019.

90 Powell, Alvin. "When Science Meets Mindfulness." *The Harvard Gazette*. April 9, 2018. https://news.harvard.edu/gazette/story/2018/04/harvard-researchers-study-how-mindfulness-may-change-the-brain-in-depressed-patients/.

91   "Benefits of Mindfulness." HelpGuide. Accessed October 4, 2020. https://www.helpguide.org/harvard/benefits-of-mindfulness.htm.

92   "Understanding the Stress Response." Harvard Medical School: Harvard Health. Updated July 6, 2020. https://www.health.harvard.edu/staying-healthy/understanding-the-stress-response

93   Huffington, Arianna. *The Sleep Revolution: Transforming Your Life, One Night at a Time.* 1 edition. New York: Harmony, 2016.

94   "Benefits of Physical Activity." CDC. Accessed Oct 3, 2020.https://www.cdc.gov/physicalactivity/basics/pa-health/index.htm; Tello, Monique. "Five Healthy Habits Net More Healthy Years." Harvard Medical School: Harvard Health. February 19, 2020. https://www.health.harvard.edu/blog/five-healthy-habits-net-more-healthy-years-2020021918907; "The Mental Health Benefits of Exercise." HelpGuide. Accessed October 3, 2020. https://www.helpguide.org/articles/healthy-living/the-mental-health-benefits-of-exercise.htm.

95   "Regain Your Confidence." Harvard Medical School: Harvard Health. June 2019. https://www.health.harvard.edu/staying-healthy/regain-your-confidence.

96   Proyer, René T., Fabian Gander, Sara Wellenzohn, and Willibald Ruch. 2013. "What Good Are Character Strengths Beyond Subjective Well-Being? The Contribution of the Good Character on Self-Reported Health Oriented Behavior, Physical Fitness, and the Subjective Health Status." *The Journal of Positive Psychology* 8: 222-232. https://doi.org/10.1080/17439760.2013.77776 7; Proctor, Carmel, John Maltby, and Alex P. Linley. 2009. "Strengths Use as a Predictor of Well-Being and Health-Related Quality of Life." *Journal of Happiness Studies* 10: 583-630. https://doi.org/10.1007/s10902-009-9181-2.

97   Confucius. *Book of Documents (Shujing).* JiaHu Books, 2013.

98   Waugh, Christian E., and Barbara L. Fredrickson. 2006. "Nice to Know You: Positive Emotions, Self-Other Overlap, and Complex Understanding in the Formation of a New Relationship." *The Journal of Positive Psychology* 1 (2): 93-106. doi:10.1080/17439760500510569.

99   Barbara L. Fredrickson. *Love 2.0: How Our Supreme Emotion Affects Everything We Feel, Think, Do, and Become.* New York: Hudson Street Press, 2013.

100 "Martin Luther King Jr." Brainy Quote. Accessed October 4, 2020. https://www.brainyquote.com/quotes/martin_luther_king_jr_403521.

101   "Giving Thanks Can Make You Happier." Harvard Medical School: Harvard Health. Accessed September 13, 2019. https://www.health.harvard.edu/healthbeat/giving-thanks-can-make-you-happier.

102   Peterson, Christopher, and Martin E. P. Seligman. *Character Strengths and Virtues: A Handbook and Classification.* Washington, DC: American Psychological Association Press and Oxford University Press, 2004.

103   "Cor." The Latin Dictionary. Accessed October 3, 2020. http://latindictionary.wikidot.com/noun:cor.

104   "Encourage." Thesaurus. Accessed October 3, 2020. https://thesaurus.plus/thesaurus/encourage.

105   Powell, Alvin. "When Science Meets Mindfulness." *The Harvard Gazette.* April 9, 2018. https://news.harvard.edu/gazette/story/2018/04/harvard-researchers-study-how-mindfulness-may-change-the-brain-in-depressed-patients/; "Benefits of Mindfulness." HelpGuide. Accessed October 3, 2020. https://www.helpguide.org/harvard/benefits-of-mindfulness.htm; Cahn, B. Rael, Matthew S. Goodman, Christine T. Peterson, Raj Maturi, and Paul J. Mills. 2017. "Yoga, Meditation and Mind-Body Health: Increased BDNF, Cortisol Awakening Response, and Altered Inflammatory Marker Expression after a 3-Month Yoga and Meditation Retreat." *Frontiers in Human Neuroscience* 11 (June). https://doi.org/10.3389/fnhum.2017.00315.

106   Neff, Kristen D., and Christopher K. Germer. 2013. "A Pilot Study and Randomized Controlled Trial of the Mindful Self-Compassion Program." *Journal of Clinical Psychology* 69: 28-44. https://doi.org/10.1002/jclp.21923.

107   Goleman, Daniel. *Emotional Intelligence: Why It Can Matter More than IQ.* New York: Bantam, 2005.

108   Goleman, Daniel. *Emotional Intelligence: Why It Can Matter More than IQ.* New York: Bantam, 2005.

109   "Emotional Intelligence." *Psychology Today.* Accessed September 1, 2019. https://www.psychologytoday.com/basics/emotional-intelligence.

110   Brown, Brené. *Daring Greatly: How the Courage to Be Vulnerable Transforms the Way We Live, Love, Parent, and Lead.* New York: Avery, 2015.

111 "For Families: 5 Tips for Cultivating Empathy." Making Caring Common Project. Harvard Graduate School of Education. Accessed October 4, 2020. https://mcc.gse.harvard.edu/resources-for-families/5-tips-cultivating-empathy.

112 "Can Relationships Boost Longevity and Well-Being?" Harvard Medical School: Harvard Health. June 2017. Accessed October 4, 2020. https://www.health.harvard.edu/mental-health/can-relationships-boost-longevity-and-well-being.

113 Saffarinia, Majid, Mohammadi, Narges, and Afshar, Hamid. 2016. "The Role of Interpersonal Forgiveness in Resilience and Severity of Pain in Chronic Pain Patients." *Journal of Fundamentals of Mental Health* 18 (4): 212-219. http://jfmh.mums.ac.ir/article_7164.html; Harris, Alex H. S., Frederic Luskin, Sonya B. Norman, Sam Standard, Jennifer Bruning, Stephanie Evans, and Carl E. Thoresen. 2006. "Effects of a Group Forgiveness Intervention on Forgiveness, Perceived Stress, and Trait-Anger." *Journal of Clinical Psychology* 62 (6): 715–33. https://doi.org/10.1002/jclp.20264; "Studies Suggest Forgiveness Has Health Benefits." National Public Radio. January 2, 2008. Accessed September 8, 2019. https://www.npr.org/templates/story/story.php?storyId=17785209

114 Lees, Adena Bank. "Forgiveness: A Path to Healing and Emotional Freedom." *Psychology Today*. November 13, 2018. Accessed September 5, 2019. https://www.psychologytoday.com/us/blog/surviving-thriving/201811/forgiveness-the-path-healing-and-emotional-freedom; Worthington, Everett L. Jr., and Michael Scherer. 2004. "Forgiveness Is an Emotion-Focused Coping Strategy That Can Reduce Health Risks and Promote Health Resilience: Theory, Review, and Hypotheses." *Psychology & Health* 19 (3):385–405. https://doi.org/10.1080/0887044042000196674.

115 Mayo Clinic Staff. "Forgiveness: Letting Go of Grudges and Bitterness." Mayo Clinic. November 4, 2017. Accessed September 8, 2019. https://www.mayoclinic.org/healthy-lifestyle/adult-health/in-depth/forgiveness/art-20047692.

116 Luskin, Frederic. *Forgive for Good*. Reprint edition. New York, NY: HarperOne, 2003.

117 Luskin, Frederic. "9 Steps." Learning to Forgive. Accessed September 6, 2019. https://learningtoforgive.com/9-steps/.

118   Su, Elizabeth. "My Mental Health Ritual: Self-Compassion and Setting Boundaries." Thrive Global. February 19, 2019. Accessed Oct 4, 2020. https://thriveglobal.com/stories/importance-setting-boundaries-mental-health/.

119   Brown, Brené. *Rising Strong: How the Ability to Reset Transforms the Way We Live, Love, Parent, and Lead.* New York: Random House Trade Paperbacks, 2015.

120   Brown, Brené. "Clear is Kind, Unclear is Unkind." Brené Brown Blog. October 15, 2018. Accessed October 9, 2020. https://brenebrown.com/blog/2018/10/15/clear-is-kind-unclear-is-unkind/

121   "Mother Teresa." Goodreads. Accessed October 3, 2020. https://www.goodreads.com/quotes/49502-i-alone-cannot-change-the-world-but-i-can-cast.

122   Fredrickson, Barbara L. *Positivity: Top-Notch Research Reveals the Upward Spiral that Will Change Your Life.* Edinburgh: Harmony, 2009.

123   Jenkinson, Caroline E., Andy P. Dickens, Kerry Jones, Jo Thompson-Coon, Rod S. Taylor, Morwenna Rogers, Clare L. Bambra, Iain Lang, and Suzanne H. Richards. 2013. "Is Volunteering a Public Health Intervention? A Systematic Review and Meta-Analysis of the Health and Survival of Volunteers." *BMC Public Health* 13 (773): doi:10.1186/1471-2458-13-773.

124   "The Healing Power of Kindness." Dignity Health. Accessed May 2, 2021. https://www.dignityhealth.org/hello-humankindness/power-of-compassion/the-healing-power-of-kindness.

125   Diener, Ed. *Happiness—Unlocking the Mysteries of Psychological Wealth.* Hoboken, NJ: Wiley Blackwell, 2008.

126   Wrzesniewski, Amy, Clark McCauley, Paul Rozin, and Barry Schwartz. 1997. "Jobs, Careers, and Callings: People's Relations to Their Work." *Journal of Research in Personality* 31 (1): 21–33. https://doi.org/10.1006/jrpe.1997.2162.

127   Csikszentmihalyi, Mihalyi. *Flow: The Psychology of Optimal Experience.* New York: Harper & Row, 1990.

128   Csikszentmihalyi, Mihaly. Flow: The Psychology of Optimal Experience. New York: Harper & Row, 1990.

129   Seligman, Martin E. P. *Authentic Happiness: Using the New Positive Psychology to Realize Your Potential for Lasting Fulfillment.* New York: Free Press, 2004.

130 Pollay, David J. "Gratitude and Giving Will Lead to Your Success." *Positive Psychology News.* June 2, 2007. Accessed October 4, 2020. https://positivepsychologynews.com/news/david-j-pollay/20070602268.

131 Yeager, John. "Make Your Goals Come Alive through Imagery." *Positive Psychology News.* April 12, 2010. Accessed October 4, 2020. https://positivepsychologynews.com/news/john-yeager/2010041210567.

132 McCraty, Rollin. "Figure 6- The Heart's Magnetic Field." Institue of HeartMath. Copyright 2009. https://www.researchgate.net/figure/The-hearts-magnetic-field-which-is-the-strongest-rhythmic-field-produced-by-the-human_fig11_293944391.

133 "New Science! It's Not Just the World Wide Web That Connects Us." HeartMath. April 1, 2018. Accessed September 8, 2019. https://www.heartmath.com/blog/articles/new-science-its-not-just-the-world-wide-web-that-connects-us/.

134 Lipton, Bruce H., *The Biology of Belief: Unleashing the Power of Consciousness, Matter, & Miracles.* Carlsbad: Hay House, 2008.

135 "Bring Your Character Strengths to Life & Live More Fully." VIA Character. Accessed June 27, 2020. https://www.viacharacter.org/.

136 "1/3 of Your Life Is Spent at Work." Gettysburg College. Accessed September 1, 2019. https://www.gettysburg.edu/news/stories?id=79db7b34-630c-4f49-ad32-4ab9ea48e72b&pageTitle=1%2F3+of+your+life+is+spent+at+work.

137 Snowdon, David. *Aging with Grace: What the Nun Study Teaches Us about Leading Longer, Healthier, and More Meaningful Lives.* New York: Bantam Books, 2002.

138 Feldman, Megan. "New Research Shows Significantly More Neural Connections Formed During Early Years Than Previously Thought." First Five Years Fund. April 4, 2017. Accessed October 4, 2020. https://www.ffyf.org/new-research-shows-significantly-neural-connections-formed-early-years-previously-thought/.

139 Helmrich, Barbara H. 2010. "Window of Opportunity? Adolescence, Music and Algebra." *Journal of Adolescent Research* 25 (4): 557-577. https://doi.org/10.1177/0743558410366594.

140   "Get Started with Design Thinking." Stanford Design School. Accessed October 4, 2020. https://dschool.stanford.edu/resources/getting-started-with-design-thinking.

141   "Get Started with Design Thinking." Stanford Design School. Accessed October 4, 2020. https://dschool.stanford.edu/resources/getting-started-with-design-thinking.

142   "Judgment." VIA Institute on Character. Accessed June 27, 2020. https://www.viacharacter.org/character-strengths/judgment-critical-thinking.

143   "Judgment." VIA Institute on Character. Accessed June 27, 2020. https://www.viacharacter.org/character-strengths/judgment-critical-thinking.

144   "The Best Ways to Strengthen Your Logical Thinking Skills." Indeed Career Guide. September 1, 2020. https://www.indeed.com/career-advice/career-development/strengthen-logical-thinking-skills.

145   "The Best Way to Strengthen Your Logical Thinking Skills." Indeed Career Guide. September 1, 2020. Accessed October 4, 2020. https://www.indeed.com/career-advice/career-development/strengthen-logical-thinking-skills.

146   "Characteristics of Strong Critical Thinkers." Insight Assessment. Accessed October 4, 2020. https://www.insightassessment.com/article/characteristics-of-strong-critical-thinkers.

147   "John Maynard Keynes Quotes." Goodreads. Accessed March 27, 2021. https://www.goodreads.com/quotes/50359-ideas-shape-the-course-of-history.

148   Covey, Stephen R. *The 7 Habits of Highly Effective People*. New York: Free Press, 1989.

149   Cameron, Julia. *The Artist's Way: A Spiritual Path to Higher Creativity*. New York: TarcherPerigee, 1992.

150   Malchiodi, Cathy. "Creativity as a Wellness Practice." *Psychology Today*. December 31, 2015. Accessed October 4, 2020. https://www.psychologytoday.com/us/blog/arts-and-health/201512/creativity-wellness-practice?amp.

151   Csikszentmihalyi, Mihaly. "Flow, the Secret to Happiness." Ted Talks. February 2004. Accessed October 4, 2020. https://www.ted.com/talks/mihaly_csikszentmihalyi_flow_the_secret_to_happiness?language=en.

152 Fredrickson, Barbara L., and Robert W. Levenson. 1998. "Positive Emotions Speed Recovery from the Cardiovascular Sequelae of Negative Emotions." *Cognitive Emotions* 12 (2): 191-220. https://doi.org/10.1080/026999398379718.

153 Fredrickson Barbara L. 2004. "The Broaden–and–Build Theory of Positive Emotions." *Philosophical Transactions of the Royal Society of London. Series B: Biological Sciences* 359 (1449): 1367–77. https://doi.org/10.1098/rstb.2004.1512.

154 Jung, Nadine, Christina Wranke, Kai Hamburger, and Markus Knauff. "How Emotions Affect Logical Reasoning: Evidence from Experiements with Mood-Manipulated Participants, Spider Phobics, and People with Exam Anxiety." *Frontiers in Psychology* 5, no. 570 (June 2014). doi: 10.3389/fpsyg.2014.00570.

155 "Get Started with Design Thinking." Stanford Design School. Accessed October 4, 2020. https://dschool.stanford.edu/resources/getting-started-with-design-thinking.

156 Dean, Ben. "Wisdom." Authentic Happiness. Accessed October 4, 2020. https://www.authentichappiness.sas.upenn.edu/newsletters/authentichappinesscoaching/wisdom.

157 Dean, Ben. "Wisdom." Authentic Happiness. Accessed October 4, 2020. https://www.authentichappiness.sas.upenn.edu/newsletters/authentichappinesscoaching/wisdom.

158 Ardelt, Monika. 1997. "Wisdom and Life Satisfaction in Old Age." *The Journals of Gerontology: Series B: Psychological Sciences and Social Sciences* 52 (1): P15–27. https://doi.org/10.1093/geronb/52B.1.P15; Baltes, Paul B., Jacqui Smith, and Ursula M. Staudinger. 1992. "Wisdom and Successful Aging." In *Nebraska Symposium on Motivation 1991: Psychology and Aging*, 123–67; *Current Theory and Research in Motivation*, Vol. 39. Lincoln, NE, US: University of Nebraska Press; Bianchi, Eugene C. *Elder Wisdom: Crafting Your Own Elderhood*. New York: Crossroad, 1994; Clayton, Vivian. 1995. "Wisdom and Intelligence: The Nature and Function of Knowledge in the Later Years." *The International Journal of Aging and Human Development*. https://doi.org/10.2190/17TQ-BW3Y-P8J4-TG40; Hartman, Pamela Sue. 2000. "Women Developing Wisdom: Antecedents and Correlates in a Longitudinal Sample." *Proquest Dissertation Publishing*. https://www.proquest.com/docview/230821396.

159   Lehrer, Jonah. "The Eureka Hunt." *The New Yorker.* July 28, 2008. http://www.newyorker.com/magazine/2008/07/28/the-eureka-hunt.

160   Lehrer, Jonah. "The Eureka Hunt" *The New Yorker.* July 21, 2008. https://www.newyorker.com/magazine/2008/07/28/the-eureka-hunt; Jung-Beeman, Mark, Edward M. Bowden, Jason Haberman, Jennifer L. Frymiare, Stella Arambel-Liu, Richard Greenblatt, Paul J. Reber, and John Kounios. "Neural Activity When People Solve Verbal Problems with Insight." *PLOS Biology* 2, no. 4 (April 13, 2004): e97. https://doi.org/10.1371/journal.pbio.0020097; Bowden, Edward M., Mark Jung-Beeman, Jessica Fleck, and John Kounios. "New Approaches to Demystifying Insight." *Trends in Cognitive Sciences* 9, no. 7 (July 1, 2005): 322–28. https://doi.org/10.1016/j.tics.2005.05.012.

161   Lehrer, Jonah. "The Eureka Hunt" *The New Yorker.* July 21, 2008. https://www.newyorker.com/magazine/2008/07/28/the-eureka-hunt; Jung-Beeman, Mark, Edward M. Bowden, Jason Haberman, Jennifer L. Frymiare, Stella Arambel-Liu, Richard Greenblatt, Paul J. Reber, and John Kounios. "Neural Activity When People Solve Verbal Problems with Insight." *PLOS Biology* 2, no. 4 (April 13, 2004): e97. https://doi.org/10.1371/journal.pbio.0020097; Bowden, Edward M., Mark Jung-Beeman, Jessica Fleck, and John Kounios. "New Approaches to Demystifying Insight." *Trends in Cognitive Sciences* 9, no. 7 (July 1, 2005): 322–28. https://doi.org/10.1016/j.tics.2005.05.012.

162   Dean, Ben. "Wisdom." Authentic Happiness. Accessed October 4, 2020. https://www.authentichappiness.sas.upenn.edu/newsletters/authentichappinesscoaching/wisdom.

163   Coleman, John. "Lifelong Learning is Good for Your Health, Your Wallet, and Your Social Life." *Harvard Business Review.* February 7, 2017. https://hbr.org/2017/02/lifelong-learning-is-good-for-your-health-your-wallet-and-your-social-life.

164   "Wilma Rudolph." Brainy Quote. Accessed October 3, 2020. https://www.brainyquote.com/quotes/wilma_rudolph_184353.

165   VIA Institute on Character. Accessed October 4, 2020. https://www.viacharacter.org.

166   "Spirituality." VIA Institute on Character. Accessed October 4, 2020. https://www.viacharacter.org/character-strengths/spirituality.

167 Walsh, Bryan. "Does Spirituality Make You Happy?" *Time Magazine*. August 7, 2017. Accessed May 10, 2021. https://time.com/4856978/spirituality-religion-happiness/.

168 "Oprah Winfrey Quotes." BrainyQuote. Accessed March 28, 2021. https://www.brainyquote.com/quotes/oprah_winfrey_757282

169 "Spirituality." VIA Institute on Character. Accessed October 4, 2020. https://www.viacharacter.org/character-strengths/spirituality.

170 Hyman, Mark. "Thoughts are Things." *Our Berkshire Times Magazine*. April 1, 2009. https://www.ourberkshiretimes.com/articles--illustration-blog/thoughts-are-things-by-dr-mark-hyman-ultrawellness-center.

171 "Steindl-Rast, David." Goodreads. Accessed October 4, 2020. https://www.goodreads.com/author/quotes/4182.David_Steindl_Rast

172 Fredrickson Barbara L. 2004. "The Broaden–and–Build Theory of Positive Emotions." *Philosophical Transactions of the Royal Society of London. Series B: Biological Sciences* 359 (1449): 1367–77. https://doi.org/10.1098/rstb.2004.1512.

173 Brown, Joshua, and Joel Wong. "How Gratitude Changes You and Your Brain" *Greater Good Magazine*. June 6, 2017. Accessed October 4, 2020. https://greatergood.berkeley.edu/article/item/how_gratitude_changes_you_and_your_brain.

174 "Awe May Promote Altruistic Behavior." American Psychological Association. May 19, 2015. Accessed June 27, 2020. https://www.apa.org/news/press/releases/2015/05/altruistic-behavior.

175 "Aurelius, Marcus. Meditations." GoodReads.com. Accessed June 22, 2020. https://www.goodreads.com/quotes/21296-dwell-on-the-beauty-of-life-watch-the-stars-and

176 Allen, Summer. "Eight Ways Awe Boosts Your Well-Being." Mindful. October 2, 2018. Accessed October 4, 2020. https://www.mindful.org/eight-ways-awe-boosts-your-well-being/.

177 Anderson, Craig L., Maria Monroy, and Dacher Keltner. 2018. "Awe in Nature Heals: Evidence from Military Veterans, at-Risk Youth, and College Students." *Emotion* 18 (8): 1195–1202. https://doi.org/10.1037/emo0000442.

178 Niemiec, Ryan M. *Mindfulness and Character Strengths: A Practical Guide to Flourishing*. Kirkland: Hogrefre Publishing, 2013.

179   Niemiec, Ryan M. *Mindfulness and Character Strengths: A Practical Guide to Flourishing.* Kirkland: Hogrefre Publishing, 2013; Niemiec, Ryan. M. 2012. "Mindful Living: Character Strengths Interventions as Pathways for the Five Mindfulness Trainings." *International Journal of Wellbeing*, 2(1), 22–33. https://doi.org/10.5502/ijw.v2i1.2.

180   Lipton, Bruce H. "Prologue." *The Biology of Belief: Unleashing the Power of Consciousness, Matter, & Miracles.* Carlsbad: Hay House, 2008.

181   Mooji. "We Are Being Offered a Higher Path." Youtube Video. April 7, 2020. https://www.youtube.com/watch?v=-FIS2B8Jwoo.

ABOUT AUTHENTIC STRENGTHS ADVANTAGE®

Our mission is helping people engage their character strengths to flourish and thrive at work, at school, in communities, and in life.

We provide transformative, evidence-based training, digital learning, coaching, certifications, and keynotes—empowering people to maximize energy, build resilience, boost well-being, and make meaningful, sustainable contributions. Visit us at AuthenticStrengths.com to take the free VIA strengths survey, and to discover your own unique strengths profile.

ABOUT THE VIA INSTITUTE ON CHARACTER

In 1998, Dr. Neal H. Mayerson and then President of the American Psychological Association, Dr. Martin E.P. Seligman, conceived a robust effort to explore what is best about human beings and how we can use those best characteristics in our lives. They launched an effort of unprecedented magnitude to lay the groundwork for the new science of positive psychology. Dr. Mayerson created a nonprofit (now the VIA Institute on Character) to do this work and provided the funding to support Dr. Seligman in orchestrating a diverse collection of scholars and practitioners who took three years to complete the development of the VIA Classification of Character Strengths and Virtues, and the VIA Surveys for adults and youth. The enormous response of people worldwide taking the survey has made it clear that VIA's work is resonating broadly and deeply.

The mission of the VIA Institute on Character is to advance the science and the practice of character strengths. The nonprofit offers the scientifically validated VIA Survey, free of charge, across the globe. Millions of people from more than 200 countries have taken the survey, now translated into many languages.

ABOUT THE AUTHOR

FATIMA DOMAN, author, speaker, and executive coach, has motivated audiences across six continents to leverage their authentic strengths for transformation. An influential voice in well-being, resilience, leadership, and positive change, she is passionate about empowering people for sustainable high performance–at work, at school, in communities, and in life. For decades, Fatima has worked successfully with Fortune 100 and Fortune 500 clients representing a variety of industries, and with educators, non-profits, and government agencies around the globe. Her books, *Authentic Strengths* and *True You* have been featured by the *Huffington Post*, *Psychology Today*, ThriveGlobal, on TV, radio, podcasts, and YouTube. Her online programs, microlearning, workshops, coach training, and certifications have been translated and licensed throughout the world.

As CEO of Authentic Strengths Advantage®, Fatima shares innovative, evidence-based tools rooted in the groundbreaking science of positive psychology–engaging people to bring out the best in themselves and in those they influence. Fatima serves as the Director of Character Strengths Certification for the VIA Premier Programs. She has also served as Co-Founder and Co-Director of Franklin-Covey's Global Executive Coaching Practice, as Faculty for the FranklinCovey/Columbia University Executive Coach Certification Program, and as manager of certification for the internationally acclaimed 7 Habits of Highly Effective People. Her post-graduate work includes an MA from California State University, an Advanced Executive Coaching Certification from the Columbia University Coaching Program, and she holds numerous academic, leadership and well-being certifications. Fatima's holistic approach to well-being includes coach certification from the HeartMath Institute, certification from the California College of Ayurveda as an Ayurvedic Yoga Therapist, and teacher certification at Yoga Alliance.

Made in the USA
Las Vegas, NV
04 July 2021

25913286R00085